Understanding
DEAFNESS
& TINNITUS

Professor Tony Wright

Published by fa
in association

IMPORTANT NOTICE

© Family Doctor Publications 2003–5
Updated 2005

Family Doctor Publications, PO Box 4664 Poole, Dorset BH15 1NN

Medical Editor: Dr Tony Smith
Consultant Editor: Mary Fox
Cover Artist: Dave Eastbury
Medical Artist: Peter Cox Associates
Design: MPG Design, Blandford Forum, Dorset
Printing: Reflex Litho, Thetford, using acid-free paper

ISBN: 1 898205 98 1

Contents

Introduction

Becoming deaf, however severe the hearing loss, can be a miserable experience. Unlike many other conditions, deafness is not immediately obvious to other people, and being unable to hear can cause many problems at work, at home and when socialising. People who have normal hearing frequently have little patience with those who do not hear so well. As it is often very difficult for deaf people to understand speech – which is perhaps the major characteristic that distinguishes us from other mammals – those who can hear give up trying to communicate with deaf people, get angry or just walk away.

When a child loses his hearing, other people may not notice until he develops a problem such as slowness in speech, a failure to learn new words, poor pronunciation, or even bad behaviour and emotional problems. Being born deaf in a hearing family raises problems, not only of detection but also of when, how and whether intervene. Being born deaf to profoundly deaf parents brings about another set of dilemmas for all those involved – often with disagreements among the various groups – as to what should be done in the best interests of the child.

Tinnitus, which can be described as hearing sounds or noises when those sounds or noises are not present in the environment, is very common and often occurs in association with deafness. The noises that affected people hear can be extremely distressing, alter their moods and behaviour, and even interfere with what hearing they do have. Tinnitus is an unseen condition, and kindness and sympathy from others are the exception rather than the rule.

Overall some degree of deafness affects one in seven of the UK population and this high figure results in hearing problems being the second most common reported disability in the UK. The hearing loss ranges from slightly hard of hearing to profound deafness, with ageing being the most common cause. Three-quarters of those with a hearing loss are aged over 60, although one child in every 1,000 is born with a significant hearing impairment. Tinnitus involves most people at some time in their lives but approximately 1 in 50 of the population have moderate or worse problems and 1 in 200 have their quality of life severely affected.

The dual aims of this small book are to bring about an understanding of the impact of hearing loss and tinnitus within the community and on the individuals who have these impairments. To do this, the book takes you through the structure of the ear and how it works, describes the different sorts of hearing loss that can occur, and how best they can be managed. It then goes on to describe the common and not so common problems that can damage hearing. The second part of the book explains what tinnitus is and current ideas about it, and suggests some ways to manage it.

Throughout this book, non-medical terms are used wherever possible for ease of reading. The first time a term is mentioned, it is followed by the medical name in brackets, for example, eardrum (tympanic membrane); this is intended to help readers who come across other texts where medical terms are used. Sometimes a wide range of names is given. This is not intended to confuse but to help those who 'surf the net' because acoustic neuromas, for example, are frequently called 'vestibular schwannomas', and a simple search can miss lots of useful information. A list of further reading and helpful contact points is included at the end of the book under Useful addresses.

THE DISABILITY DISCRIMINATION ACT

The Disability Discrimination Act 1995 (DDA) aims to reduce discrimination against deaf people in employment and in access to goods and services. It applies only to severely or profoundly deaf people who can prove that their deafness has an adverse effect on their daily life. It does not apply to mild or periodic hearing loss.

A disabled person must not be treated less favourably by an employer or service provider than someone who is not disabled would be treated in the same circumstances. The DDA covers anything that is related to employment (such as the offer, terms and benefits of employment) and opportunities for promotion. However, it does not cover employers with fewer than 15 staff. If a deaf person feels that he or she has been discriminated against, he or she should seek legal advice as soon as possible (for example, through their local Citizens Advice Bureau). More information about the DDA can be obtained by calling the DDA Helpline for an information pack or visiting their website – see the Useful addresses at the end of the book.

KEY POINTS

✓ Deafness is very common: one in seven of the UK population has some degree of deafness

✓ Deafness affects speech, language and communication

✓ Deafness can cause isolation

✓ Deafness has a major impact on the community

✓ Tinnitus is very common

✓ Tinnitus often occurs with deafness

The structure of the ear

The human ear is one of the more remarkable parts of the human body, not only because of the beauty and unlikelihood of its structure, but also because of its remarkable sensitivity to sounds. From an anatomical point of view, the ear is conventionally and conveniently divided into three parts: the outer, the middle and the inner ears.

THE OUTER EAR

The outer ear comprises the pinna (auricle), which is made of a convoluted plate of flexible cartilage that extends as a nearly closed tube one-third of the way down the ear canal. This outer third, which is about eight millimetres (one-third of an inch) long, has small hairs that point outwards to form a line of defence against small animals creeping in. The roots of the hairs produce oils and these mix with the secretions from nearby sweat-like glands to form the basis of wax. The deep two-thirds of the ear canal (16 millimetres/two-thirds of an inch long) has a bony wall lined with thin and rather fragile skin which is devoid of glands. At the far end of the ear canal and stretched across it is the eardrum (tympanic membrane), which forms the boundary between the outer and middle ears.

THE MIDDLE EAR (TYMPANUM)

The eardrum is a circle of thin skin about eight to nine millimetres (one-third of an inch) in diameter. Despite its name, it is not flat like the skin of a drum, but is slightly conical with the curved sides sloping inwards. The eardrum has three layers.

The outer layer
In contact with the deep ear canal, the outer layer is covered with a thin layer of skin.

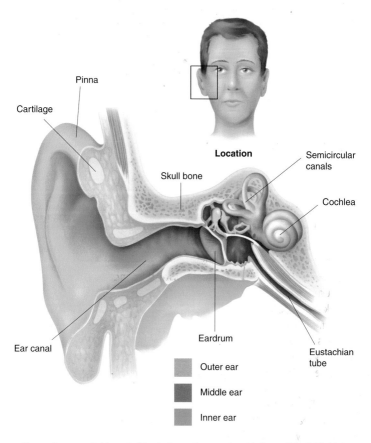

Pinna

Cartilage

Location

Skull bone

Semicircular
canals

Cochlea

Ear canal

Eardrum

Eustachian
tube

Outer ear

Middle ear

Inner ear

The ear is a remarkable part of the body sensing sound and balance. It is divided into three parts: the outer, middle and inner ears.

The inner layer

The inner layer is in continuity with the lining of the middle ear, and consists of rather flat cells that have the ability to transform into the type of cells that line the nose and sinuses. Following infection, chemical irritation – such as tobacco smoke – or allergy, these cells alter and produce mucus which flows into the middle ear.

The middle layer

The middle layer of the eardrum is very important and consists of elastic fibres arranged both like the spokes of a wheel (radial fibres) and in circles (circumferential fibres), so

THE OUTER EAR

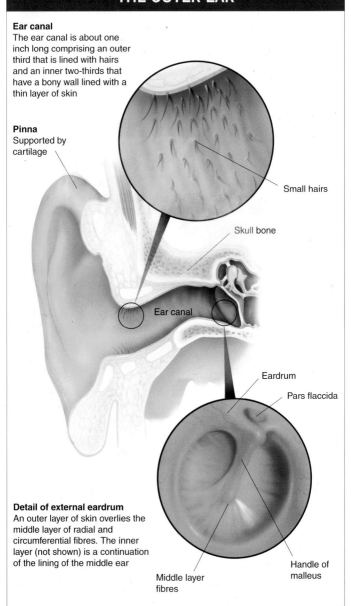

Ear canal
The ear canal is about one inch long comprising an outer third that is lined with hairs and an inner two-thirds that have a bony wall lined with a thin layer of skin

Pinna
Supported by cartilage

Small hairs

Skull bone

Ear canal

Eardrum

Pars flaccida

Detail of external eardrum
An outer layer of skin overlies the middle layer of radial and circumferential fibres. The inner layer (not shown) is a continuation of the lining of the middle ear

Middle layer fibres

Handle of malleus

that this layer is like a sprung trampoline net. The larger lower three-quarters of the eardrum (the pars tensa) is tense and absorbs sound. The smaller upper portion of the membrane is more floppy because the fibres of the middle layer are not organised in regular patterns, and this region is called the pars flaccida. The middle ear itself (the tympanum) lies deep to the eardrum and is an air-filled space that holds three small bones (ossicles), which connect the eardrum to the inner ear.

These bones are called the hammer (malleus), anvil (incus) and stirrup (stapes) because of their resemblance to these objects. The hammer has a handle and a head and the handle lies within the layers of the eardrum. The head of the hammer sits in the upper part of the middle-ear space called the attic (epitympanum) and is connected by a joint – just the same as any other joint in the body – to the rather bulky body of the anvil. From the anvil, a long strut (the long process) descends back into the middle ear proper and is connected to the head of the stirrup. The two arches (crura) of the stirrup join the footplate, which sits in a small (3 mm × 2 mm) hole in the skull called the oval window (fenestra ovalis). This is the opening into the fluid-filled space of the inner ear. Just below the oval window is another small hole into the inner ear called the round window (fenestra rotunda). A thin membrane closes this and, when the footplate of the stirrup moves 'in and out', the round window membrane moves 'out and in' because the fluid in the inner ear transmits the pressure changes.

The hammer and anvil are supported in the middle ear by several membranes and ligaments, which minimise their weight, allow them to move easily and bring them a blood supply. Unfortunately, this leaves only a small space for the passage of air from the middle ear to the attic.

Running through the middle ear is the facial nerve (nerve VII or the seventh nerve). This nerve leaves the brain and has to pass through the skull on its way to supply the muscles of facial expression, that is, muscles for frowning, winking, smiling, scowling, and so on. The nerve lies in a thin bony tube and runs horizontally from the front to the back of the middle ear just above the oval window and stirrup, before it turns downwards to leave the base of the skull. The nerve then turns forwards to reach the face. The facial nerve is therefore relatively vulnerable in diseases of the middle ear and, indeed, in middle-ear surgery itself. A facial palsy results in one side of the face being paralysed, so that the face

THE MIDDLE EAR

The middle ear is an air-filled space that holds three small bones (ossicles) which connect and transmit vibration from the eardrum to the inner ear.

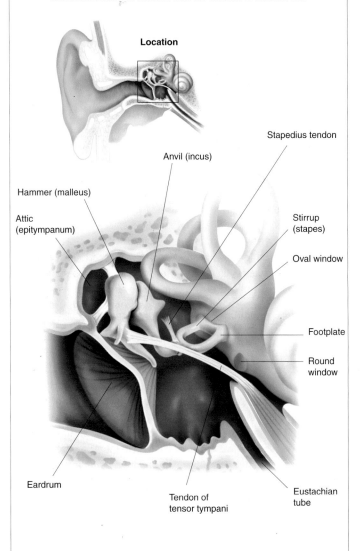

Location

Stapedius tendon

Anvil (incus)

Hammer (malleus)

Attic (epitympanum)

Stirrup (stapes)

Oval window

Footplate

Round window

Eardrum

Tendon of tensor tympani

Eustachian tube

droops and fails to move. Smiling results in a scowl and drinking in dribbling, and the eye fails to close on blinking.

Running through the eardrum is the nerve that carries taste from the front two-thirds of the tongue (the chorda tympani nerve). This nerve is on its way to join the facial nerve in the middle ear where it 'hitch-hikes' a lift back to the brain.

Finally, there are two small muscles in the middle ear. The one at the front (tensor tympani) is attached at the top of the handle of the hammer and tenses up the eardrum when swallowing activates it. The function of this muscle is not clear but it may be to make eating and swallowing a less noisy event.

The muscle at the back of the middle ear (stapedius) arises near the facial nerve, is supplied by it and attaches to the head of the stirrup. It responds to loud sounds by contracting and stiffening the chain of small bones, and possibly reduces transmission of prolonged and potentially damaging, loud sounds to the inner ear.

THE INNER EAR (LABYRINTH)

The inner ear is probably the most remarkable intricate piece of the body. It makes hearing possible by converting sound into electrical impulses that then travel along the hearing nerve (the acoustic nerve or auditory nerve) to the brain. The inner ear also plays a major role in balance. The balance portions of the inner ear (vestibular labyrinth) can detect acceleration of the head in any direction whether in a straight line (linear) or twisting and turning (angular). The electrical signals that arise in response to head movement pass along the balance nerve (vestibular nerve), which in due course joins with the hearing nerve to form a single bundle (stato-acoustic, vestibulo-acoustic or eighth nerve, nerve VIII) which then enters the brain.

The portion of the inner ear that actually hears is the cochlea. This is a hollow coiled tube set in the very dense bone called the bony labyrinth (part of the petrous [rock-like] temporal bone). This tube is filled with fluid, which is much the same as general body fluid (lymph) and that which surrounds the brain (cerebrospinal fluid – CSF). This inner-ear fluid is called perilymph. Inside the perilymph is another coiled triangular-shaped tube called the cochlear duct (scala media), which contains the all-important 'hair cells' – these convert sound into electricity. These hair cells are arranged in two groups that follow the coils of the cochlear duct and spiral upwards from base to apex. There is a single row of inner hair cells (IHCs), which lie closer to the core of the cochlea (modiolus), and

THE INNER EAR – BALANCE

The balance portions of the inner ear can detect acceleration of the head in any direction, whether in a straight line or twisting and turning.

Semicircular canals

The three semicircular canals lie at right angles to each other. The canals are fluid filled and each contains a sensory organ called a crista, which is capped by the cupula

When the head moves, the fluid in the canals displaces the cupula, stimulating the nerves in the crista

Location

Vestibule

There are two fluid-filled chambers each containing a sensory organ called a macula. When the head moves, the gelatinous membrane of the macula is displaced, stimulating the nerve

Vestibular nerve

Cupula at rest

Cupula

Crista

Fluid

Sensory hairs

Displaced cupula

Fluid pressure

Bent hairs

Macula at rest

Sensory hairs

Gelatinous membrane

Displaced macula

Displaced membrane

Pressure

Bent hairs

three or four rows of outer hair cells (OHCs), which are further away. In a healthy young human ear there are about 3,500 IHCs and about 12,000 OHCs. Each hair cell has a cluster of small rigid hairs (stereocilia), which project from the thicker upper surface of the cell into the special fluid that fills the cochlear duct. This fluid is called endolymph and is remarkable in that it has a strongly positive electrical charge associated with it – about 80 millivolts – and is rich in potassium, a metallic element.

The hair cells in their rows are grouped together with their supporting cells in the organ of Corti. This is a small ridge that sits on a thin, very flexible membrane called the basilar membrane. The basilar membrane forms the floor of the triangular cochlear duct. The sloping roof is another very thin membrane (Reissner's membrane) and the side wall is a thickened region rich in blood vessels (the stria vascularis). This structure is responsible for maintaining the composition of the rather unusual and very important endolymph.

Adjacent to the base of the hair cells are the nerves that carry impulses to the brain (the afferent nerves). At least 90 per cent of these nerves come from the inner hair cells, despite their smaller number. Each inner hair cell has about 10 nerve endings attached to it and there are, therefore, about 30,000 nerve fibres in the acoustic nerve.

The outer hair cells have nerves attached to them but most are nerves coming from the brain (the efferent nerves), whose function is described later.

The hearing nerves travel inwards, along with the balance and facial nerves, through a canal in the inner part of the skull (variously called the internal auditory meatus [IAM], internal auditory canal [IAC] or porus acousticus) to reach the brain stem. This part of the brain deals with lots of automatic functions such as pulse, blood pressure, general alertness, balance, and so on.

About half of the hearing nerves from each ear cross over to the other side of the brain stem and then, on both sides, the nerves pass up the brain stem through the mid-brain, eventually to reach 'consciousness' in what is called the cortex of the brain. For hearing, this conscious region is located in the temporal lobe portion of the brain, which lies on each side of the head just above the ear.

SOUND AND HOW THE EAR WORKS

Sound

Sound travels as small waves of pressure through the air at a speed of about 343 metres per second

THE INNER EAR – SOUND

The inner ear is probably the most intricate piece of the body. It makes hearing possible by converting sound into electrical impulses, which then travel along the hearing nerve to the brain.

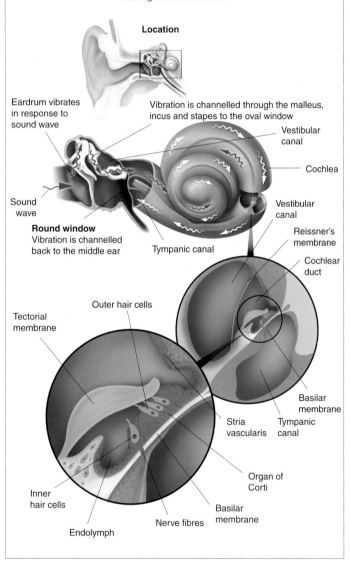

Location

Eardrum vibrates in response to sound wave

Vibration is channelled through the malleus, incus and stapes to the oval window

Vestibular canal

Cochlea

Sound wave

Round window
Vibration is channelled back to the middle ear

Vestibular canal

Reissner's membrane

Cochlear duct

Tympanic canal

Outer hair cells

Tectorial membrane

Basilar membrane

Stria vascularis

Tympanic canal

Organ of Corti

Inner hair cells

Nerve fibres

Basilar membrane

Endolymph

(740 miles per hour). The waves of sound are rather like ripples on the surface of a pond spreading out after a stone has been thrown in. These waves have pitch (frequency) and that is the number of crests that pass a point in a second. Pitch is measured as 'cycles per second' (cps) which is now more commonly written as hertz (Hz) after Heinrich Rudolf Hertz (1857–1894), a pioneering scientist who worked on theories of light and electricity; 261 Hz is equivalent to middle C on the piano. One thousand cycles per second (1,000 cps) is one kilohertz (1 kHz).

Sound waves also have intensity and, when the comparison is made with ripples on the pond, this equates to the volume of the wave. In real life, it is easier to measure the pressure of the wave rather than its intensity and this pressure is measured in units called pascals (Blaise Pascal [1623–1662] was, among other things, a mathematician and physicist of genius working on statistics, probability and geometry, and atmospheric pressure). One

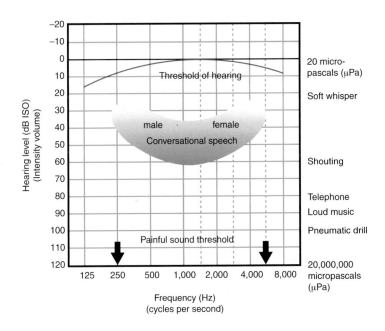

The human ear is very versatile and able to differentiate a wide variety of sounds by intensity (volume) and frequency (pitch).

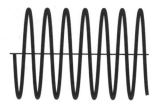

High pitch
High intensity (volume)

High pitch
Low intensity (volume)

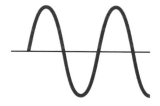

Low pitch
High intensity (volume)

Low pitch
Low intensity (volume)

Sound travels as waves through the air rather like ripples on the surface of a pond. These waves have pitch (number of wave crests) and intensity (height or volume of the wave).

pascal is rather large for sound pressure measurements so that micropascals (μPa), that is, one-millionth of a pascal, tend to be used.

The quietest sound that the average healthy 18 year old, without previous ear problems and with normal eardrums, can hear has a pressure of 20 micropascals (20 μPa). This level forms the basis for measuring the pressure of other commonly heard sounds in our environment.

The range of pressures that the ear can hear is enormous. The quietest, just detectable sound may be 20 μPa, but a jet engine heard close by has a level of 20,000,000 μPa. For convenience these levels are recorded as decibels (dB) after Alexander Graham Bell (1847–1922), teacher of the deaf and inventor of the telephone, the audiometer and gramophone, who derived a convenient way of expressing this huge range of sound pressures.

HOW HEARING WORKS

Sound waves are partly collected by the pinna, which in humans has only

THE RANGE OF PRESSURE THAT CAN BE HEARD BY AN UNDAMAGED EAR

The ear is capable of hearing a wide range of sounds. The ratio of the sound pressure of the lowest limit that undamaged ears can hear to that which causes permanent damage is more than a million. The decibel scale is very useful in discussing sound because it is a logarithmic scale, which can be used to describe very big ratios in volume with numbers of modest size.

Decibels	Micropascals	Typical perception
0 dB	20 µPa	The quietest sound a healthy 18 year old can hear
20 dB	200 µPa	A very soft whisper
50 dB		A softly spoken voice
60 dB	20,000 µPa	A shout
70 dB		A noisy motor bike in a narrow street
80 dB	200,000 µPa	
90 dB		An over-loud discotheque club or an illegally noisy factory because it is at this level that sound damages the ears
120 dB	20,000,000 µPa	The noise of a jet engine

a limited function. You will have noticed how dogs prick up their ears in response to an interesting sound; this enables them not only to hear better but also to localise the source of a sound more accurately. In humans, the convolutions of the pinna do help a little in both respects, but complete loss of the pinna only reduces the hearing by a few decibels, although sound localisation is impaired.

The ear canal not only protects the eardrum from direct damage, but also has a role in hearing. The resonance properties of a tube that is open at one end and closed at the other result in sounds being enhanced over a certain frequency range at the closed end of the tube. The common example of resonance happens when you blow across the top of an empty bottle to produce a note. If the bottle is then partly filled with liquid, the note changes as the resonance properties change. For the dimensions of the human ear, this enhancement is most marked in the range 1,500–6,000 Hz which just happens to include most of the frequencies used for speech and sorting out one complex sound from another – for example, speech from background noise.

The large area of the eardrum, which is not rigid but flexible and buckles slightly to help absorb energy, now collects the sounds. The hammer, anvil and stirrup transfer this sound energy to the relatively small area of the oval window.

This system, which comprises the large flexible eardrum linked by a chain of bones with a small lever action to the inner ear, is really quite efficient in converting airborne sound waves into sound waves in the fluids of the inner ear.

Normally, when sound hits the surface of a liquid, 99.5 per cent or more is reflected. The operation of the middle-ear mechanism results in about 50 per cent of the sound reaching the eardrum being transferred to the inner ear.

As sound waves hit the perilymph beneath the footplate, they create a wave that travels up and around the cochlea. This travelling wave builds up to a maximum for each particular pitch and then rapidly falls away to nothing. The location of the peak of the wave varies at different pitches: for high-pitched sounds, the wave peaks near the base of the cochlea, whereas for low-pitched sounds this peak is near its apex.

As this pressure wave passes through the cochlea, there is movement of the thin basilar membrane and, along with it, the organ of Corti containing the hair cells. Overlying the hair cells is a gelatinous membrane called the tectorial membrane. One edge of this is attached to the bony core at the centre of the cochlea (the modiolus); the other is loosely attached to the organ of Corti outside the outermost outer hair cell. The tips of the hairs of the OHCs are lightly embedded in the under-surface of the tectorial membrane whereas the tips of the IHCs (which, as mentioned earlier, give rise to most of the nerve fibres) do not reach the tectorial membrane and stand free in the endolymph.

As the travelling wave reaches

THE MECHANISM OF HEARING

Outer ear
Pinna helps collect and channel sound into the ear canal, which also enhances sound quality

Middle ear
Eardrum vibrates in response to sound waves and transmits the sound energy through the three small bones to the oval window

Inner ear
Vibrations from the oval window pass to the fluid, creating a wave that travels up and around the cochlea back to the round window, which disperses the vibration back to the middle ear

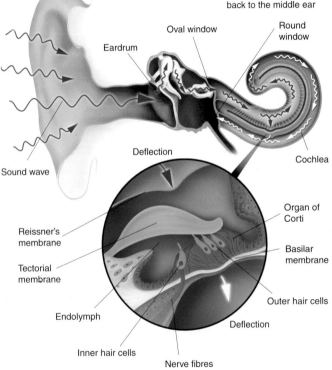

Oval window

Eardrum

Round window

Deflection

Cochlea

Sound wave

Reissner's membrane

Tectorial membrane

Endolymph

Inner hair cells

Nerve fibres

Organ of Corti

Basilar membrane

Outer hair cells

Deflection

Organ of Corti
The pressure wave deflects the vestibular membrane and so the basilar membrane activates the hair cells of the organ of Corti, creating nerve stimuli

its peak, the OHCs near this peak give a small, physical 'kick' to enhance the movement of the basilar membrane. This internal amplifier causes the endolymph to squirt towards the hairs of the IHCs. If the movement of fluid is great enough, the hairs are deflected and very small channels open up somewhere near the tips of the hairs. The potassium in the endolymph can now flood down through these small channels, being propelled by the very strong positive electrical charge of the endolymph into the bodies of the IHCs. Here the influx of potassium alters the hair cell membrane and small parcels of chemicals are released from the base of the hair cell, causing the

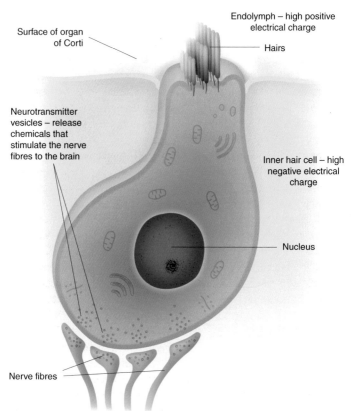

Surface of organ of Corti

Endolymph – high positive electrical charge

Hairs

Neurotransmitter vesicles – release chemicals that stimulate the nerve fibres to the brain

Inner hair cell – high negative electrical charge

Nucleus

Nerve fibres

An inner hair cell found within the organ of Corti. When the endolymph is disturbed by sound deflecting the basilar membrane, small channels open up somewhere near the tips of the inner hair cells. This allows the positive charge into the body of the inner hair cell, stimulating the nerve cells at its base to send an impulse to the brain.

nearby nerves to become active and send pulsed signals towards the brain.

The signals pass from one relay station to the next in a regular fashion and have complex interactions in the brain stem. About one-fifth of a second after detection, electrical signals reach the auditory areas of the brain (auditory cortex of the temporal lobes) and sounds are perceived.

At each step, the system is set to maximise sensitivity to sound. There is the very well-balanced middle-ear mechanism, which generates the pressure changes in the cochlea that result in the complex travelling wave; this, in turn, depends on the delicate fine structure of the cochlea. There is the highly unusual fluid named the endolymph and a quite remarkable internal cochlear amplifier. Why so? Quite simply, hearing is an important and efficient early warning system. Without good hearing most mammals would find it difficult to survive.

THE MIDDLE EAR, EUSTACHIAN TUBE AND MASTOID

In order to hear, creatures living on land need to have an eardrum with air on both sides to collect airborne sound and transfer it onwards to the inner ear. Reptiles, birds and mammals all have the same system,

although the numbers of bones are different in the three groups and birds have only one strut-like bone between the eardrum and inner ear.

In mammals, the middle ear is lined with a tissue that is rather like the lining of the nose, with mucus-producing glands and cells with a surface covered by moving flexible hairs or cilia – not to be confused with the stereocilia of the hair cells, which are different structures altogether and which are not mobile. The middle ear is, therefore, an air-filled space, lined with living tissue capable of producing both debris from dead surface cells and mucus from the glands. This creates two problems: first, clearing the debris and mucus and, second, a more subtle but very important problem. Oxygen is absorbed from the air in the middle ear into the blood vessels running through its lining, in much the same way that oxygen is absorbed in the lungs. Some carbon dioxide is given off from those same blood vessels into the air in the middle ear, but overall the effect is a drop in middle-ear pressure as more oxygen is removed than carbon dioxide produced. With atmospheric pressure outside the eardrum, something has to 'give' and the only thing that can move is the eardrum. This would be pushed inwards by the external pressure and the eardrum would then stop working normally. Eventually the

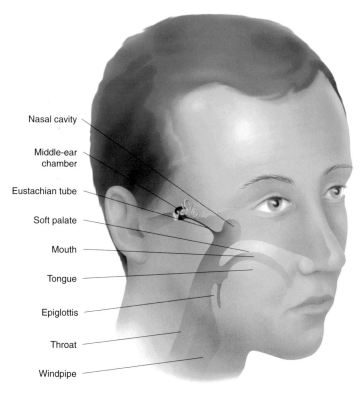

Nasal cavity

Middle-ear chamber

Eustachian tube

Soft palate

Mouth

Tongue

Epiglottis

Throat

Windpipe

The middle ear is connected to the nasal cavity via the eustachian tube. This tube allows the middle ear to maintain an equal pressure with the outside and replenish the cells of the middle ear with oxygen.

whole middle ear would collapse and a significant hearing loss would develop.

When working properly, the eustachian tube prevents both these problems. This tube runs forwards and inwards from the front wall of the middle ear to open into the back of the nasal cavity above the soft palate (the nasopharynx). The end nearer the nose is soft and

flexible, and opens when you swallow or yawn. Although we do not know precisely how this mechanism works, when the eustachian tube opens, enough air enters the middle ear to replenish the oxygen that has been absorbed and so keep the middle-ear pressures close to atmospheric. It has been calculated that only one or two millilitres of air per ear per day

– that is, less than half a teaspoon of air – are necessary to maintain proper ventilation of the middle ear, but without this the middle ear fails to perform properly.

The eustachian tube is also the conduit along which the cilia move the mucus produced in the middle ear to the back of the nose, where it can be swallowed. This thin film of mucus, carrying the debris produced in the middle ear, is moved along the floor of the eustachian tube with air passing above it to reach the middle ear from the nose. Thus, the two functions of ventilation and self-cleansing are achieved when the system is working properly. Unfortunately, in humans, the mechanism is rather fragile and often fails to work adequately, possibly because of the shape of the skull that is needed to accommodate the large brain.

There is also an extension of the air-filled spaces of the middle ear backwards into the mastoid bone. You can feel this as a rounded bump if you put your hand to the back of your ear. The mastoid bone should be hollow, with the air-filled spaces broken up by small and incomplete bony partitions rather like a honeycomb. The average mastoid has an air volume of about 15–20 millilitres (three to four teaspoons) and this helps to buffer pressure changes in the middle ear and reduce adverse effects on the tympanic membrane. People with small mastoid air spaces seem to be at a much greater risk of developing middle-ear and mastoid disease. As yet, we do not fully understand whether it is middle-ear and mastoid disease that cause the failure of the mastoid to develop, or whether a small size reduces the pressure buffer and therefore causes the development of disease. The probable answer is that it will be a bit of both.

✓ The ear comprises outer, middle and inner ears

✓ The outer ear collects sounds and enhances the speech frequencies at the eardrum

✓ The middle ear conducts the sound energy to the fluid of the inner ear

✓ The inner ear contains the sensory hair cells that convert sound energy into electrical messages that pass to the brain

✓ The outer hair cells act as an internal amplifier and also provide clarity and discrimination

✓ The whole system is incredibly sensitive and therefore very delicate

Different types of deafness

As we have seen in the preceding chapters, hearing is a complex affair, which can therefore go wrong in many different ways. Some processes we understand and some we do not. However, it is possible to classify the different sorts of deafness, because they fall into two major groups based on which side of the footplate of the stirrup the problem occurs. In other words: is the problem located in the ear canal or middle ear or, is the inner ear, cochlear nerve or auditory perception area of the brain not working? The first type of hearing loss is called a conductive loss because it is a failure of sound conduction to the inner ear; the second type is called a sensorineural or perceptive loss. Sometimes, individuals have both problems; this is referred to as a mixed loss.

Hearing losses can turn up in many ways. Individuals can be born with a hearing loss when it is called a 'congenital loss'. This loss can be conductive or sensorineural or, more rarely, a mixed loss. Alternatively, the condition causing the hearing loss may be inherited but does not have to be present at birth. Otosclerosis (see page 55) is a good example of a hereditary conductive loss. Finally, the condition can be acquired during life and noise-induced hearing loss is an example of an acquired sensorineural loss whereas a perforated eardrum is an acquired conductive loss.

Overall conductive, sensorineural and mixed losses can belong

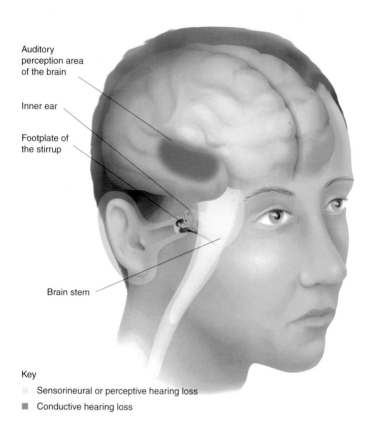

Auditory
perception area
of the brain

Inner ear

Footplate of
the stirrup

Brain stem

Key

Sensorineural or perceptive hearing loss

Conductive hearing loss

Different forms of deafness fall into two major groups depending on which side of the
footplate of the stirrup the problem occurs. Sometimes individuals have both
problems – this is termed a mixed loss.

to any of the three categories, which indicate how they arise – that is, congenital, hereditary or acquired. The importance of this classification is that the detection of the condition, the impact of the problem, the management of the individuals concerned and the potential outcomes vary enormously, depending on the origin of the hearing loss.

KEY POINTS

✓ Deafness can arise from problems in the outer, middle and inner ears as well as with the auditory nerve and brain

✓ Deafness from the outer and middle ears is called a conductive loss

✓ Deafness from the inner ears or the acoustic nerve is called a sensorineural or perceptive loss

✓ Hearing loss from changes in the brain is called a central loss

Assessing hearing loss

Before it is possible to manage hearing loss, this loss has to be detected and assigned to the appropriate categories of conductive, sensorineural or mixed hearing loss. The basic test is the pure-tone audiogram (PTA). Other common tests are also described here, but there is a whole science of hearing tests, which is beyond the scope of this book.

THE PURE-TONE AUDIOGRAM

The aim of this test is to determine the quietest sound levels that an individual can just detect for a range of notes across the frequency keyboard. This level is called the 'hearing threshold', which represents the volume of sound that can just be detected at any particular pitch. The range of the test is

CLASSIFICATION OF HEARING LOSS

Quietest sound an individual can just detect	Classification of hearing
20 dB or less	Normal hearing
25 dB or more	Mild hearing loss
45 dB or more	Moderate hearing loss
65 dB or more	Severe hearing loss
85 dB or more	Profound hearing loss

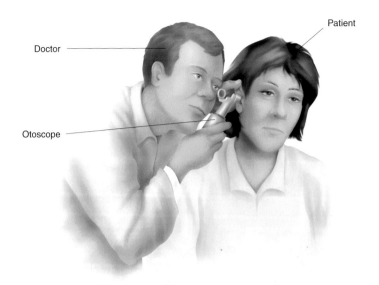

An otoscope can be used to examine the ear canal and outer surface of the eardrum.

generally spread over the five octaves from 250 Hz to 8,000 Hz. An octave is a doubling of frequency, that is, from 250 to 500 Hz then from 500 to 1,000 Hz, from 1,000 to 2,000 Hz, and so on. Although each octave is a doubling of frequency, the brain hears each octave as equal steps.

The test starts at one frequency, typically 1,000 Hz. The person being tested wears standardised headphones connected to an audiometer. The sound is directed to one ear at a time and is played at moderate volume, at say 60 dB, for several seconds. If the tone is heard, the person, who should not be facing the tester, presses a response button and holds it down while he or she is hearing the sound, so that the tester knows that there is a positive response. The volume is then reduced in 10-dB steps and the process repeated until the person no longer detects the sound. The tester then increases the volume in 5-dB steps until the sound is detected again and then down in 10-dB steps and up in 5-dB steps until the sound is detected three times out of five on the 'ascent'. The decibel level is then entered on the audiogram chart and the process repeated for other frequencies up and down the scale, normally at 250, 500, 1,000, 2,000, 4,000 and 8,000 Hz for routine testing. If the person is involved in a claim for damages or there are abnormalities, 3,000 and 6,000 Hz and possibly other frequencies are tested as well.

Although 0 dB is the average lower limit of hearing for healthy 18 year olds, the upper limit of normal is taken as 20 dB. Lower limit hearing thresholds worse than 20 dB – that is, 30, 40, 50 or more – suggest a reduced hearing level (HL).

BONE-CONDUCTION TEST

Testing with headphones gives 'air conduction' (AC) levels and tests the whole system from the external ear canal to the auditory perception regions of the brain. This test does not distinguish whether a loss is conductive, sensorineural or mixed. To do this the inner ear must be tested and this is achieved by assessing 'bone conduction' (BC). In this test a small vibrator, which is

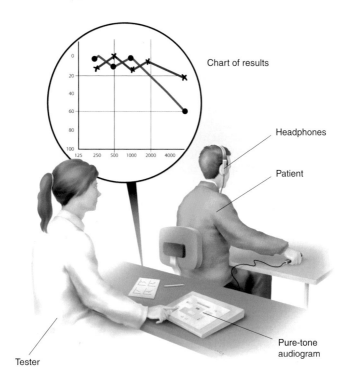

Chart of results

Headphones

Patient

Pure-tone audiogram

Tester

The pure-tone audiogram measures how loud a sound has to be for you to hear it. The sound is directed to one ear and reduced in steps until the person can no longer hear it. The volume is then raised in steps and lowered again until the threshold is confirmed.

also connected to the same audiometer, is pressed firmly against the skull usually over the mastoid prominence. Vibrations from the device enter the skull and are transmitted directly to the inner ear, bypassing the ear canal and middle ear. This was how Beethoven, who must have had a severe conductive deafness, was able to hear, by pressing his head via a stick to his piano.

The same testing process as for the pure-tone audiogram is repeated using the vibrator, giving bone-conduction thresholds that represent the hearing level in the cochlea, acoustic nerve and brainstem pathways up to the level of the auditory cortex. Again, normal bone-conduction thresholds are taken as being better than (that is, less than) the 20 dB level, with 0 dB being the average normal level.

If the air conduction shows poor hearing, but the bone conduction is normal, there is an 'air–bone gap' and the hearing loss is conductive. If

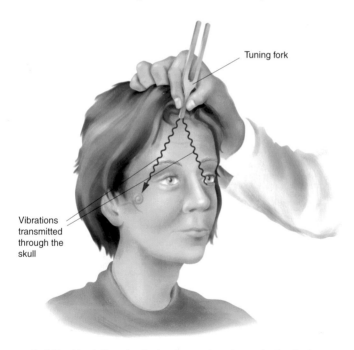

Tuning fork

Vibrations transmitted through the skull

To distinguish whether a hearing loss is sensorineural or conductive, the inner ear must be tested by 'bone conduction'. This principle can be demonstrated by placing a tuning fork on your forehead. Vibrations enter the skull and are transmitted directly to the inner ear.

PURE-TONE AUDIOMETRY (PTA)

Pure-tone audiometry (PTA) gives information on the functionality of the auditory pathway. The test determines the quietest sound levels that an individual can just detect for a range of notes across the frequency keyboard. This level is called the 'hearing threshold'. The following charts illustrate the results that could be expected for four different hearing conditions.

A chart representative of a 'normal' healthy ear.

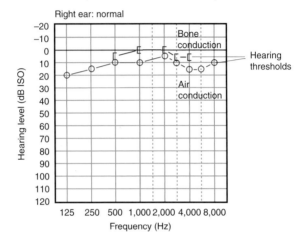

A chart typical of noise-induced hearing loss.

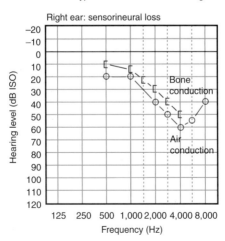

PURE-TONE AUDIOMETRY (PTA) (contd)

Testing with headphones gives 'air conduction' (AC) levels. 'Bone conduction' (BC) levels are found using a small vibrator, which is also connected to the same audiometer, pressed firmly against the skull, usually over the mastoid process. Vibrations from the device enter the skull and are transmitted directly to the inner ear, bypassing the ear canal and middle ear.

Results that might be expected with a perforated eardrum.

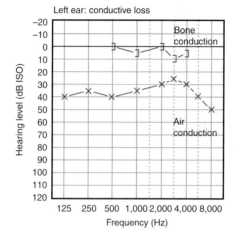

Left ear: conductive loss

This pattern might be found in otosclerosis with additional changes in the inner ear.

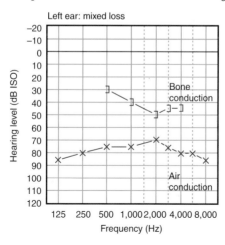

Left ear: mixed loss

both the bone conduction and air conduction are similarly poor and there is no significant air–bone gap then the loss is 'sensorineural'. If there is both poor air conduction and poor bone conduction and a significant air–bone gap – that is, 15 dB or more – the loss is mixed.

There are some practical difficulties with the PTA that can make interpretation impossible if a test is not conducted with great care. The most common one occurs with bone-conduction sound applied by the vibrator to one side of the head. This sound vibrates the whole skull and is transmitted to both the inner ears with only a 5-dB reduction in sound energy occurring across the skull. Thus, if one ear is being tested and the inner ear on that side is damaged, the sound will be detected by the other good ear and 'heard'. This gives a false impression of the hearing level in the tested ear and can result in serious errors in diagnosis. A masking sound, usually in the form of white noise – a shushing sound – has to be applied to the non-test ear to prevent this kind of mistake happening.

Another problem occurs when one ear has a large conductive loss but good bone conduction, that is, a good sensorineural reserve, and the other ear has a serious sensorineural loss. It may be impossible to get enough masking into the non-test ear with the conductive loss to make even a reasonable assessment of the true bone-conduction levels in either ear.

Once it has been decided that the loss is sensorineural, there are several techniques for deciding where the problem lies.

AUDITORY EVOKED POTENTIAL TESTING

Once the cochlea has detected an incoming sound, it converts it to an electrical signal, which travels along the nerves to the areas of the brain responsible for perception. The whole electrical journey takes only about one-fifth of a second. It is possible to detect the various electrical steps along this route by placing sensitive electrodes on the scalp and over the mastoid region. The signals occur whenever the cochlea detects sounds and so the individual's active cooperation is not needed.

Unfortunately the auditory signals are extremely small and are swamped in the generalised electrical activity of the brain, the nerves and the muscles. To overcome this problem, we can present a short 'click' stimulus to the ear and then record on a computer the electrical activity from the electrodes for a short while, say 10 milliseconds – that is, ten-thousandths of a second – after. This time interval is then divided by the computer into even smaller intervals or 'bins'. During the ten milliseconds of recording, the activity of the cochlea and the responses of the acoustic nerve are measured. The test is therefore called electrocochleography. If the recording time is lengthened the activity in different parts of the auditory pathway – the brain stem and auditory cortex – can be assessed.

As the signal arrives at the computer, it is allocated bit by bit to successive 'bins'. The electrical signal at each point is either positive or negative and has a certain voltage, so that the bin accumulates a plus or minus value. The process is restarted with the computer returning to the first bin before the next click is made. The process is repeated again and again in this time-locked fashion.

The background electrical activity of the brain, nerves and muscles is more or less random and so, after a time, there will be about equal numbers of positives and negatives of a range of voltages arising from these structures allocated to each bin. When these random elements of the signal are all added up they more or less cancel each other out.

This leaves the auditory signal intact because, at any point of collection, the auditory signal is always positive or always negative

and these values accumulate with successive time-locked samples. The whole process is called auditory evoked potential (AEP) testing. Most computer programs now have the ability to work out the signal-to-noise effect and can cancel out unduly noisy signals so that the best result is achieved in the least time. Depending on the time window during which data are collected, different parts of the auditory system can be assessed.

Electrocochleography (ECoG), brain-stem (BAEP) or cortical (CAEP) auditory evoked potentials all give different information about different parts of the auditory pathway. What is very important about this form of measurement technique is that the tester does not need the cooperation of the person to obtain a response. This whole group of tests is therefore called objective audiometry, as opposed to the term 'subjective audiometry' which is used for pure-tone testing and for other tests needing the person's response. BAEP and CAEP can detect a response without the person's help and can also be used to create the equivalent of a pure-tone audiogram without the person having to respond.

This is achieved in a similar fashion to the pure-tone audiogram described above. The testing starts with a loud click, or better still by using a short burst of a pure tone

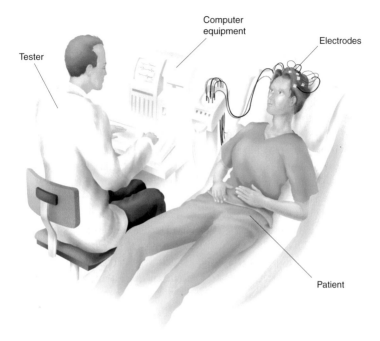

It is possible to monitor the electrical signals, produced after the cochlea has detected sound, passing to the area of the brain responsible for the perception of sound. The process is called auditory evoked potential (AEP) testing.

(that is, a sound of a single frequency) usually of 1,000, 2,000 or 3,000 Hz, to get a response. Then the volume is gradually reduced until the electrical response to click or the tone burst disappears. This level is taken as being close to the true hearing level (hearing threshold).

This technique is very useful in testing those people who, for some reason, are unable to produce a reliable conventional pure-tone audiogram. This might include those claiming compensation for injury who may inadvertently exaggerate their hearing loss; those who feign a hearing loss as an excuse for criminal activities; and a few people with psychological problems that show up as deafness. One big group who cannot respond is made up of babies and young children, and it is just this group in whom it is essential to be certain whether the hearing is intact and, if not, how bad it is.

DISTRACTION TECHNIQUES
Conventional hearing testing of babies who can sit up and hold up

their heads has relied on what are called 'distraction techniques'. The child sits on a parent's lap and faces one of the testers who engages his attention. The second tester stands behind the child to one side with some means of producing sound. Nowadays, calibrated devices producing pure tones of different frequencies are in common use. When a sound is made at about a metre from the child's ear and at the same level, the child will go still, turn his eyes to one side or even turn his whole head if he is aware of the sound. This is taken as a positive response. A failure to do this is taken as a negative response, although too much concentration on the first tester, tiredness and a variety of other factors can conspire to mean that the test does not really prove that the child has poor hearing.

Other sounds such as a spoon in a cup, rattles or squeakers can be used and are good at producing a response from children. However, with each of these test items, a range of frequencies is produced and a deaf child with residual low-tone hearing can often give a response to the low-tone elements of the test sound and thereby give a

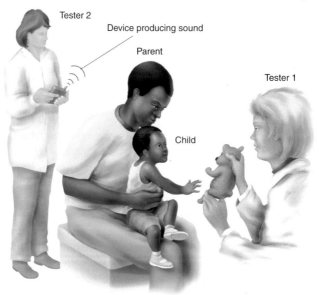

Tester 2
Device producing sound
Parent
Tester 1
Child

Distraction tests are suitable for testing, simply, the hearing of young babies who are able to sit up and hold up their heads. One tester maintains the child's attention. The second tester stands behind the child with a device that produces a sound. The child's reaction to the sound is observed.

reassuring but false test result. Good teamwork between the two testers is also needed to obtain reliable results. When a child consistently fails to respond to such tests, he will require further assessment, often by some form of brainstem auditory evoked potential (BAEP) testing as described on page 33. This would need to be performed under general anaesthetic or sedation.

There are variations of the distraction test, including visual reinforcement audiometry where a correct response is 'rewarded' by a cuddly toy in a darkened box being lit up for a moment or two. After the age of about two and a half years, performance tests can be introduced. Here, the child performs an action such as putting a toy brick in a box in response to sound and usually with a reward for a correct answer.

OTOACOUSTIC EMISSION TESTING

Distraction techniques cannot be used with a newborn baby and routine auditory evoked potential testing as a screening procedure is simply not feasible to detect those with a moderate or more severe loss because it takes time, considerable skill and a placid, sleeping or anaesthetised baby.

You may recall, from the description of how the cochlea

works, that the outer hair cells become active when the crest of the travelling wave reaches them. The outer hair cells respond in a mechanical fashion by shortening or lengthening, which somehow brings about mechanical amplification of the sound wave. This then results in the bending of the hairs of the inner hair cells and the production of cochlear nerve impulses.

Whatever the exact mechanism of the cochlear amplifier, the process is not 100 per cent efficient, and some of the mechanical energy generated by the outer hair cells travels back down the cochlea and moves the footplate of the stapes from the inside. This movement is transmitted through the ossicular chain back to the eardrum and thence to the ear canal. In the 1970s, David Kemp (now Professor of Auditory Biophysics at University College London) predicted that these cochlear 'echoes' should exist and eventually was able to detect them in the ear canal by using computer-averaging techniques. These signals are not, however, electrical in nature, but are sound waves coming back out of the cochlea in response to sounds going in. In a normal ear, they bear a resemblance to the in-going sound, hence the term 'cochlear echo'.

Eventually, these cochlear echoes acquired the more descriptive title of otoacoustic emissions (OAEs). For OAEs to be present, the cochlea has to be healthy with an intact set of outer hair cells (OHCs), and the middle ear also has to be normal. In general, the hearing level has to be 30 dB or better for an OAE response to be detected. Thus, if there is a response, the hearing is normal. The test is quick, repeatable, non-invasive and does not require skilled technicians or scientists to perform it and,

importantly, the equipment is no longer expensive.

The test involves introducing a gentle sound into the outer ear canal with a small probe. A fraction of a second later, the probe picks up an 'echo' returning from the cochlea. The echo is present in all hearing people and can be measured by computer. If the echo is absent, this may indicate that a child's hearing mechanism is not working properly and further tests will be needed.

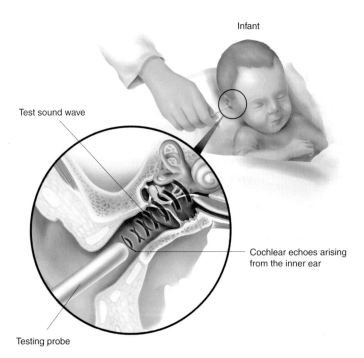

Infant

Test sound wave

Cochlear echoes arising from the inner ear

Testing probe

Distraction tests cannot be used with a newborn baby. Otoacoustic emission testing detects the presence of 'cochlear echoes', which indicate that the middle and inner ears are healthy. The test is well suited for an infant as it is quick, simple and non-invasive.

In many countries, routine screening of all newborn babies in hospitals is required by law and those who fail the test go on to further screening and assessment. It seems much more sensible to be aware of and manage a problem as early as possible rather than to allow it to be discovered later when the remedy may be too late to benefit the child.

Universal screening of hearing for babies has finally been accepted in principle in the UK. However, the resources to fund the implementation of a screening programme are not yet available, despite comprehensive American studies showing that the technique is effective, efficient and economical.

TYMPANOMETRY (IMPEDANCE AUDIOMETRY)

As well as being able to test the hearing level, it is often very helpful to know about the state of the middle ear. Tympanometry can help in this respect and relies on the fact that the eardrum, although good, is not a perfect absorber of sound. Sounds put into the canal are partly absorbed and partly reflected by the eardrum, and a microphone can detect this reflected sound. If an airtight probe containing a small loudspeaker, a small microphone and a fine tube connected to an air pressure pump is put into the ear canal, some of the sound-conducting properties of the middle ear can be measured

Raising or lowering the pressure in the ear canal stretches the eardrum a little, making it less efficient so that more sound is reflected. In more technical terms, the impedance increases. The microphone can detect this change as more sound is reflected from the stretched eardrum and the change in impedance can be calculated. If the pressure in the ear canal is gently changed from normal atmospheric pressure to a slightly increased pressure, and then gradually reduced through normal to a low negative pressure, the changes in the efficiency of the eardrum can be measured continuously and plotted on a small graph. This is the tympanogram.

A normal tympanogram has a bell-shaped curve with the peak of the curve close to the normal atmospheric pressure (type A curve). A low, flat trace occurs when the middle ear is full of fluid and the eardrum is very inefficient (type B curve). If there is air in the middle ear, but the pressure is reduced because of eustachian tube inadequacy, the peak of the trace is shifted to the low-pressure region of the graph and is usually reduced in height (type C curve). This indicates that to get the eardrum into its most efficient unstretched state a low pressure in the ear canal

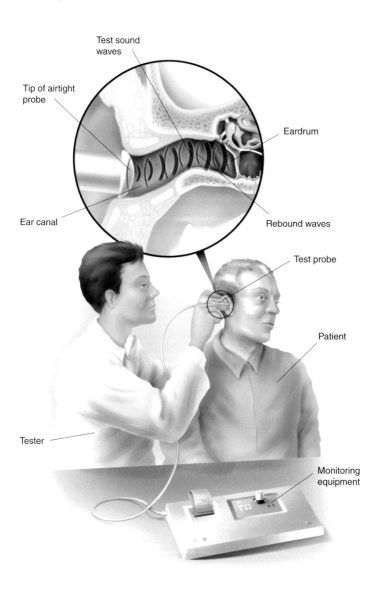

Test sound waves

Tip of airtight probe

Eardrum

Ear canal

Rebound waves

Test probe

Patient

Tester

Monitoring equipment

Tympanometry measures the sound-conducting properties of the middle ear. The pressure in the ear canal is raised and lowered while sound waves are projected into the ear. The sound reflected from the eardrum is measured and plotted on a graph.

has to be created to match the low pressure in the middle ear. This test therefore also gives us a measure of the pressure in the middle ear.

If the bones in the middle ear are broken or not connected to each other, as can happen after a head injury, then a very tall, peaked tracing is obtained. If the bones are stuck together, as in otosclerosis, the peak of the trace is often reduced in height, although still in the normal pressure region.

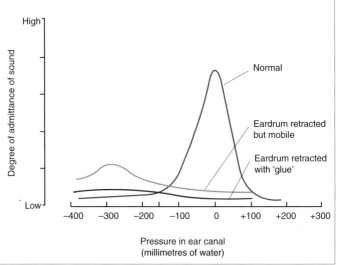

TYMPANOMETRIC CURVES

Sound put into the ear canal is partly absorbed and partly reflected. The more stretched the eardrum the more sound is reflected. Tympanometry measures this degree of reflection, which is a good indication of the state of the middle ear.

KEY POINTS

✓ Hearing tests can be subjective – relying on the individual's own response – or objective – when the individual does not have to make a decision because the response is automatic

✓ The pure-tone audiogram is the basic test for assessing hearing

✓ Hearing loss can be mild to moderate, severe or profound

✓ Hearing tests can determine whether there is a problem – where the problem arises – although it cannot say exactly what is causing the trouble

What causes deafness?

CONGENITAL AND HEREDITARY DEAFNESS

Development of the ear

During a baby's development, the outer and middle ears and the inner ear arise from quite different and separate structures and at different times. Given the complexity of the system, it is remarkable that they manage to join up and work at all.

During the nine months of development and growth, the fertilised egg goes through many stages. After implantation in the lining of the uterus, pre-embryonic and then embryonic development begin. During this hectic phase, which lasts about eight weeks, all the major organs and systems are created. The embryonic period finishes as the heart begins beating and the fetal period is said to start. Over the next seven months until birth, no new types of tissue develop, but there is considerable growth and reorganisation of what is already present.

The outer and middle ears develop from grooves that arise on the outside of the embryo, and from pouches or clefts that develop on the inside in the tubular space, which will later form the mouth, nose, throat and gullet. This region is called the primitive foregut. Four or, sometimes, five pairs of these grooves and clefts develop on each side of the embryo. (In fishes these grooves and clefts will become the gills.) In mammals, only the first pouch and cleft are of any significant size and the junction of the outside and inside persists and eventually forms the eardrum. The external groove becomes the ear canal and the internal cleft becomes the middle ear, the mastoid and the eustachian tube.

Beneath the skin at the outside of the ear canal, six small mounds of cartilage make their appearance and grow, move and join to form the external ear or pinna.

Between each of the grooves and clefts is a bar of cartilage that runs around the side of the foregut. These bars are called the branchial arches and will later develop into important structures. The first arch cartilage becomes the lower jaw and the hammer, anvil, and probably the arch of the stirrup. The second arch becomes what is called the hyoid bone, which is the horseshoe-shaped bone just above the voice box (larynx). The lower arch cartilages end up forming the larynx. Each arch has a major nerve arising from the brain associated with it. These nerves are called the

cranial nerves and there are 12 nerves arising on each side.

The first arch, which forms the lower jaw, has the fifth nerve (nerve V, also called the trigeminal nerve) running in it to supply, among other things, the muscle associated with chewing. The second arch has the seventh nerve (nerve VII or facial nerve) running through it, on its way to supply the muscles that surround the various openings in the head – eyes, nose, mouth and ears. These muscles eventually become those that give expression to the face.

As the fetus grows, big changes occur in this region, and the middle ear and eustachian tube expand and

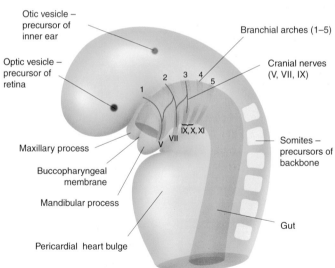

Diagram of the 'primitive foregut' of a developing mammal. This stage of development is never actually seen as depicted because development occurs at different speeds and at different times in each region.

force the facial nerve to take its peculiar, tortuous course through the middle ear.

What can go wrong during development?

As can be imagined, all sorts of mistakes and errors can occur during this period of rapid development. Probably the most common problem to involve the hearing is a failure of the ear canal to develop; this is called an atresia. If the tube forms properly but becomes narrowed or closed by some other problem such as an infection, this is called a stenosis. Congenital atresia of the ear canal occurs in about one baby in every 15,000. Fortunately, most of these involve only one ear so that the child can still hear. Babies who are born with atresias affecting both ears not only have immediate hearing problems, but often also have other abnormalities affecting the face and head.

The most common abnormality is probably the Treacher Collins syndrome. A syndrome is a collection of medical problems that regularly occur in individuals to form a recognised pattern. The Treacher Collins syndrome includes low-set, malformed external ears, atresia of the ear canal, under-developed cheeks, jaws and palates, and unusual eyelids that are inclined downwards at their inner edges. A baby born with this condition will have a normal intellect. There are many different syndromes that can involve the outer ear, the middle ear or both.

In the middle ear the ossicles can be malformed or fused together and, if the ear canal is normal, it may be possible to repair the defect surgically to restore the child's hearing. However, advances in hearing aid technology and the introduction of bone-anchored hearing aids (see page 82) have made many operations for congenital ear disease redundant, given their risk of serious complications and the imperfect hearing results that most surgeons achieve.

The inner ear develops quite separately from the outer and middle ears and initially arises from the surface of the embryo, just behind the developing eye, as a flat area called the otic placode. This then sinks into the surface. As it does so the edges turn in on themselves and join together to form a small hollow ball – the otocyst. A remarkable series of changes occurs with the semi-circular canals developing from one side of the otocyst at about day 35 of the fetus' life. Soon after, the cochlea starts to develop as a small bud at the base of the opposite side. This enlarges and coils to form the two and a half turns of the adult human cochlea. The hair cells start to develop within the organ of Corti

Factors in the mother-to-be
- Drugs that are toxic to the ear (ototoxic) such as the aminoglycoside antibiotics

- *Infections caught during pregnancy*
  Rubella (German measles), toxoplasmosis, cytomegalovirus, measles, chickenpox, herpes, HIV, syphilis

- *Factors at birth (perinatal)*
  Severe jaundice, oxygen deprivation

- *Infection of the newborn baby*
  Meningitis, encephalitis, septicaemia

at about 11 weeks and, by 25 weeks, the whole labyrinth is full size and complete, as are the eardrum, middle ear and ossicles. Nerves from the nearby brain stem grow out to make contact with the hair cells of hearing and balance to form the acoustic and vestibular nerves. The soft tissues surrounding the labyrinth condense into a tough bony shell to protect the delicate structures inside.

The developing labyrinth is susceptible to damage during development so that the baby may be born with some hearing loss. This is called an acquired congenital sensorineural hearing loss. Common causes are infections caught by the child's mother, such as German measles (rubella) and toxoplasmosis (*Toxoplasma* is a parasite found in cat faeces) during the first three months of her pregnancy. Problems around birth, especially severe oxygen deprivation (perinatal asphyxia), can also cause damage to the inner ear and/or the auditory pathways in the brain. This can also occur if the baby develops prolonged and severe jaundice (kernicterus). This used to be fairly common when the mother's and baby's blood groups were different, so that with successive pregnancies the mother started to react against the baby with serious results, especially liver damage and subsequent jaundice. The most common problem was with the so-called rhesus blood groups when mother was rhesus negative and the baby rhesus positive. Fortunately, modern antenatal care has made this particular problem much less common.

One of the many deformities that can occur during development and without any obvious cause is Mondini's deformity, in which there is a malformed, sac-like cochlea with wide semicircular canals and only islands of low-frequency hearing left. Other children are born with a profound deafness and none of the obvious causative factors listed above, nor a family history of inherited deafness and a cochlea that looks normal on X-rays. In these cases, it is presumed that there has been a failure of the organ of Corti to develop. Provided that they have an acoustic nerve, which can be seen by magnetic resonance imaging (MRI), these children may benefit from a cochlear implant (see page 84).

Inherited deafness

Hereditary hearing losses were first studied systematically by Sir William Wilde in 1853 (William Wilde was Oscar Wilde's father and a famous Dublin ENT surgeon). He recognised that inheritance was a major cause of congenital deafness and noted that intermarriage increased the risk of the problem. It was not until the Franciscan monk Gregor Mendel published his studies on inheritance in 1865 that the patterns of hereditary deafness began to be understood. Autosomal dominant sensorineural hearing loss accounts for about 30 per cent of children who are born with an inherited deafness. The term 'autosomal dominant' means that one particular gene carries the defect and, if the child inherits that gene from either parent, he or she will be deaf. Sometimes deafness is the only evidence of a gene defect and at present 13 genes have been located that are responsible for this type of problem, which is called non-syndromic because there are no other features associated with it.

Syndromic dominant hearing losses have deafness as part of an overall pattern of features; Waardenburg's syndrome is a typical example. Affected individuals have a white streak in the hair at the forehead and/or white eyebrows, different coloured eyes and a sensorineural hearing loss.

Most of the remaining causes of inherited deafness are autosomal recessive, which means that the defective gene has to be inherited from both parents for the child to be deaf. The deafness is generally more severe than in the autosomal dominant cases. Diagnosis is often difficult or impossible if there is no family history, but if there are affected brothers or sisters or if the parents are related this will provide support for the diagnosis. Once again there are syndromic and non-syndromic types. There are at least 17 genes that are responsible for non-syndromic autosomal recessive hearing loss, and the incidence is thought to be about one in 3,000 births. The hearing losses, as in the autosomal dominant cases, can be progressive and there may be a delay in the onset of the loss. This may be difficult to detect if hearing screening by otoacoustic emission testing has not been performed shortly after birth (see page 36).

A typical example of the syndromic autosomal recessive losses is Usher's syndrome, which probably accounts for about 10 per cent of people with a hereditary loss. Changes in the eye are a part of this syndrome, with night blindness being noticed first, followed by a patchy loss of vision (scotomata) and then tunnel vision with only a small central area of vision left. This part of the condition is called retinitis pigmentosa, and the combination of poor vision and a severe sensorineural loss is particularly disabling and very upsetting because the visual loss can begin in the teens. Although there is no specific cure for a hereditary hearing loss, a correct diagnosis is important for adequate counselling of the parents – who are usually devastated and often distraught with unnecessary guilt – and the child concerned. It is important to make use of all the skills and technology that are becoming increasingly available. Difficult decisions have to be made about what is likely to be in the best interests of the child.

GLUE EAR

One of the most common conditions affecting children's hearing is the presence of fluid in the middle ear. Normally, the middle ear is air filled. The air-filled spaces of the middle ear are connected with the back of the nose by the narrow eustachian tube. The role of the eustachian tube is twofold:

1. To transfer air to the middle ear. This is necessary because oxygen from the middle ear is absorbed into the blood through the lining of the middle-ear spaces. This would result otherwise in a reduction in pressure in the middle ear, which would cause the eardrum to stretch inwards, and so impair hearing.

2. To allow the mucus that is normally produced in the middle ear to escape into the nose and thereby prevent accumulation.

After colds many people suffer from temporary failure of the eustachian tube to clear the mucus produced by the lining of the middle ear in response to the viral

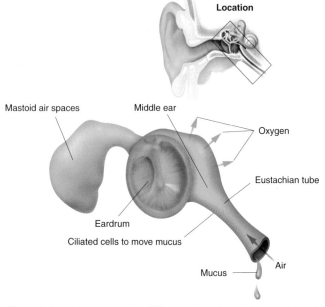

Location

Mastoid air spaces

Middle ear

Oxygen

Eustachian tube

Eardrum

Ciliated cells to move mucus

Mucus

Air

The eustachian tube connects the middle ear with the back of the nose. It functions to allow oxygen into the middle ear and mucus produced in the middle ear to drain away into the nose.

infection. The result is a blocked, sometimes uncomfortable ear, with a loss of hearing and frequently a sense of being able to hear your own voice inside your head (autophony). This condition is called acute secretory otitis media and usually gets better in a few weeks without treatment.

In children who have frequent colds, or who have allergies or are sensitive to environmental pollutants, such as cigarette smoke, the continuing production of mucus is possible. If this fails to clear, the middle-ear system becomes clogged with mucus that is 'locked in'. Eliminating it is rather like trying to get treacle out of a tin can when there is only one small hole in the lid. When the fluid has been present for three months or more, the condition is called 'glue ear' – in other words it is a chronic (long-lasting) secretory otitis media. This condition is also called otitis media with effusion (OME, especially in America) or occasionally middle-ear effusion (MEE). The condition affects boys more than girls and is worse in the winter than in the summer. It occurs at any age in childhood, but there seem to be two peaks in the incidence at two years and five years, although the reasons are unclear

The fluid in the middle ear causes a moderate hearing loss which is rarely worse than a hearing level of 45 dB. However, with this comes difficulty in learning to speak if the condition starts when the child is very young, or a failure of the growth of language skills and development of vocabulary if the condition starts later.

Behaviour can also change and children can lack concentration, and become angry or aggressive, or withdrawn and introspective. They can invent imaginary friends as companions. Established glue ear is rarely painful, but the stagnant fluid in the middle ear can become infected so that severe pain and fever develop until the eardrum bursts and a mucoid, stringy pus discharges (acute suppurative otitis media).

Most children with established glue ear eventually recover without treatment, the number affected reducing by half with every three to four months that pass. However, not all the children recover spontaneously and there is a small group, of perhaps five per cent of those who start out with glue ear, who continue to have problems with changes in the eardrum, which can result in long-standing and serious ear disease (see Perforated eardrums and Cholesteatoma later)

Treatment of glue ear is difficult and sometimes contentious. As most children recover without any treatment, some doctors suggest that all that is necessary is to give the children hearing aids and treat infections as they arise. Although this may be effective for many children, there is that small group who will suffer permanent and irreversible damage to the eardrum and middle ear if this 'watch and wait' approach is adopted. Trials of medical management suggest that, in some allergic children, nasal steroids used as drops or sprays can help reverse the condition, but this is not always effective.

Surgical intervention consists of re-ventilating the middle ear by using a small ventilation tube (grommet) about 1.5 millimetres in diameter. This is inserted through a small slit made in the eardrum (a myringotomy) and allows air into the middle ear so that mucus can, in turn, drain down the eustachian tube. Ventilation also seems to help the lining of the middle ear return to normal. Sometimes grommet insertion is accompanied by removal of the adenoids, because in about 25 per cent of children this helps speed up the natural resolution.

A recent Medical Research Council trial (TARGET trial) has

GLUE EAR

Normally the middle ear is air filled. If the eustachian tube fails to function normally, the middle ear becomes clogged with mucus. If this persists for more than three months, the condition is called 'glue ear'.

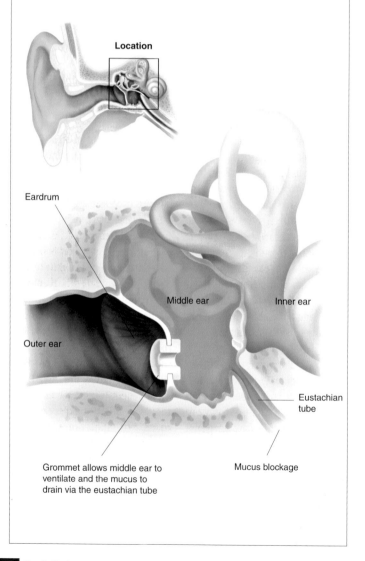

Location

Eardrum

Middle ear

Inner ear

Outer ear

Eustachian tube

Grommet allows middle ear to ventilate and the mucus to drain via the eustachian tube

Mucus blockage

shown that an adenoidectomy has a very strong, positive benefit to the outcome of managing glue ear and should probably be undertaken at the first intervention.

For children with established glue ear, the only treatment that immediately restores the hearing is the insertion of a functioning grommet. There is no substantial evidence that having a grommet with a hole in it, in the eardrum, makes the child more prone to middle-ear infections after swimming. Most ENT surgeons, however, advise parents to be careful when washing their child's hair because soapy water has a low surface tension, which makes water 'thinner' so that it is easier for dirty, soapy water to get into the middle ear and cause problems. There are no restrictions on aeroplane flights for a child who has grommets in place and a fully ventilated middle-ear space makes flying easier.

The eardrum is a living, growing part of the body and slowly moves the grommet and eventually ejects it into the ear canal after six to nine months. Some grommets come out earlier and some last longer – sometimes much longer. Having a grommet in the eardrum may have minor side effects. When the grommet is eventually ejected, a few children are left with a hole that fails to heal. In the early stages, this is not such a bad thing because the perforation is acting as a grommet. In the long term and when the child has outgrown the 'glue ear phase' of his or her life, the hole can become a problem and may need repair if it continues to cause infections when water gets into the ear.

The eardrum can also become slightly stretched by having a grommet in place and it responds by laying down chalky deposits in the areas of tension. These chalky white accumulations are called tympanosclerosis and, unless they are extremely extensive (which is rare), they have no effect on the hearing or the ability to cope with pressure changes.

Sometimes the glue ear can recur after the grommet is ejected, when a second set of grommets is needed if the hearing is affected or the eardrum is undergoing changes that could result in long-term problems. A small group of children require the repeated insertion of ventilation tubes and eventually it will be necessary to decide whether a more permanent type of tube is required. This is not needed very often, but when the eardrum is becoming thinned and indrawn or is becoming stuck down to the underlying anvil and stirrup, this remedy usually helps prevent long-term damage to the eardrum and can sometimes reverse changes that have occurred.

PERFORATED EARDRUMS

Changes in the middle ear become an increasing cause of moderate-to-severe conductive deafness as people get older. Although glue ear is the most common cause of a conductive deafness in childhood, most, but not all, children grow out of the condition to be left with normal middle ears.

Some children will have had repeated middle-ear infections with an excruciatingly painful build-up of pus in the middle ear and an associated high fever. Eventually, the eardrum bursts, the pain is relieved and a sticky, mucoid pus discharges from the ear canal. The condition settles and the hole in the eardrum usually heals. The new eardrum, however, usually has only two layers (as opposed to the normal three) because the middle fibrous layer is either not formed or incomplete. The intact but weakened eardrum can be the source of many problems later in life.

Sometimes the eardrum fails to heal and a perforation is left. This problem can occur after ear infections at any age. Perforations can also be the result of damage to the eardrum from the unwise use of cotton buds in the ear or from abrupt pressure changes such as can occur during diving accidents, and even from syringing ears with eardrums weakened from earlier infections. Simple perforations

cause a conductive loss up to 40 dB depending on the size and site of the hole. They can also be the cause of recurrent ear infections after colds or when dirty water from baths, the sea or swimming pools gets into the ear.

Recurrent ear infections can eventually alter the lining of the middle ear and mastoid, so that, instead of the discharge occurring occasionally, the lining of the middle ear continues to produce a mucoid discharge that becomes infected from time to time. This is now called chronic suppurative otitis media (CSOM). If antibiotics and careful clearance of the middle ear using a fine suction tube and a microscope to provide both magnification and illumination of the ear fail to settle the problem, surgery to close the perforation is usually required. At surgery the unhealthy lining of the middle ear and mastoid is usually removed to ensure that the eardrum returns to a normal state.

Sometimes, the repeated infections result in damage to the tip of the long arm (the long process) of the anvil so that the ossicular chain is disrupted. When this happens the hearing worsens and a 60-dB conductive loss develops. This form of severe conductive loss can also occur after a major head injury that is severe enough to shake the anvil out of position. Disruption of the anvil from the stirrup is the most common form of ossicular discontinuity and, provided the eardrum is intact, it can usually be repaired by removing the anvil, refashioning it, and then replacing it between the head of the stirrup and the inside of the handle of the hammer. This procedure is called an ossiculoplasty and, although the individual's own bone is the best material, artificial bone can now also be used with good results.

Some people grow into adulthood with eardrums that are scarred but not perforated and with eustachian tubes that do not work well. This is probably the most difficult group of middle-ear problems for ENT surgeons to manage. As the eustachian tube is not working properly, there is intermittent low pressure in the middle ear, which eventually results in the scarred segment of eardrum retracting and, rather like Clingfilm, attaching itself to the underlying structures (this is called an adhesive otitis media). For many years this may go unnoticed (that is, it is asymptomatic), but eventually the ossicles become stuck down and usually the long arm of the anvil disintegrates.

The eardrum can also get itself trapped in some of the deeper recesses of the middle ear and this can result in both a recurrent, often foul-smelling discharge and cholesteatoma formation (described below). For recurrent infections with their associated conductive loss, successful surgery is difficult because the true cause of the problem – that is, eustachian tube insufficiency – is impossible to 'cure'. Some form of artificial ventilation to the middle ear has to be created along with the repair to ensure that the problem does not recur. At present, surgical techniques fall short of perfection, but are usually good at restoring dry healthy middle ears, although the restoration of normal hearing is more elusive.

CHOLESTEATOMA

One common and potentially dangerous condition of the middle ear and mastoid is called cholesteatoma. The name of the condition does not do much to explain what is taking place in the ear, or what damage can be caused by the failure to diagnose and treat this disease.

The ear canal and eardrum are covered by skin. One of the functions of skin is to protect the body against wear and tear, and to form a waterproof layer called the epidermis. To achieve this, skin grows continually from its lower levels to the surface and, as the dividing cells approach the surface of the skin, they die and shrink to form a waterproof layer. This surface layer is made waterproof by the presence of a protein called 'keratin'. The dead surface layers of skin cells are continually shed with wear and tear and, on the scalp, these scales of discarded skin are commonly known as dandruff. This pattern of growth is found all over the surface of the body. However, if this process were to happen in the ear canal it would rapidly become blocked with layers and layers of dead keratinised skin cells.

To overcome this problem, the skin of the eardrum and ear canal has evolved, or been given, the special property of migration. In other words, the skin of the eardrum and ear canal grows outwards from the middle of the eardrum, along the ear canal to the external opening of the ear. The outer third of the ear canal has small hairs in it and the oil that is secreted from the little glands in the hair roots, along with modified sweat from the small sweat glands, mixes with the scales of dead skin to form wax. Wax protects the ear because it kills many common and unpleasant bacteria and fungi, and generally stops insects and other foreign bodies from inadvertently travelling down the ear canal.

The skin of the eardrum can fairly easily become misplaced and find itself in the middle ear. This can arise from problems in childhood

when the eustachian tube fails to function normally and results in considerably reduced pressures in the middle ear and mastoid. The normal air pressure in the external ear canal forces the eardrum skin to bulge into the middle ear as a 'retraction pocket'. This is made easier if middle-ear infections have damaged and thinned the eardrum so that it loses its resilience. At first the eardrum skin is still able to migrate out of the shallow pocket in the usual manner, but if the pocket becomes too deep the skin is unable to grow around the edge of the pocket and the surface layers of dead skin begin to accumulate.

This accumulation of dead skin forces the underlying live skin cells to expand, so that layer upon layer of dead cells accumulate and are surrounded by a very thin layer of still living and actively growing eardrum skin. This growth is called a cholesteatoma.

As the cholesteatoma expands into the middle ear and mastoid, it comes into contact with nearby structures and eventually erodes them. This can result in several possible problems arising. Damage to the bones in the middle ear can lead to deafness, but this can also result from erosion of the inner ear (labyrinth), which is usually associated with dizziness because of damage to the balance portions of the inner ear. The facial nerve, which supplies the muscles of facial expression, runs through the middle ear and invasion of this by cholesteatoma can cause a droopy face. Above the middle ear is the brain and, if it is invaded by the cholesteatoma, this can cause major neurological conditions including epilepsy and even death. However, the usual way in which cholesteatoma makes its presence known is with a foul-smelling discharge resulting from infection of the masses of dead skin.

Treatment of cholesteatoma is usually by some form of surgery, which is primarily aimed at making the ear safe by removing disease. Modern surgical techniques also aim at making the ear dry and attempt to maintain or even improve the hearing. Surgery involves risks, but in competent hands the chance of complications occurring from surgery is much less than allowing the disease to progress unchecked.

OTOSCLEROSIS

For a person to hear properly, the middle ear has to function normally. First, the eardrum has to be intact, with air at the same pressure on either side of it. Second, the ossicles (hammer, anvil and stirrup) that connect the eardrum to the inner ear by way of the oval window have to be properly connected and mobile. One of the most common

problems to affect the ossicular chain is otosclerosis. This is a peculiar condition without any known cause, which affects more women than men and tends to run in families, so that several generations on the female side of the family may have it. However, new cases occur frequently in people without any family history. The condition almost invariably involves both ears in due course, although a few people do develop otosclerosis in one ear yet have perfect hearing in the other.

What happens in otosclerosis is that the bone surrounding the oval window, in which sits the footplate of the stirrup, starts to enlarge and thicken. The footplate of the stirrup is held in the oval window by a thin, tough elastic membrane called the annular ligament. When normal, this arrangement allows the sound waves collected by the eardrum to be efficiently and effectively transferred to the fluids of the inner ear. As over-growth of the new bone progresses and involves the annular ligament, the mobility of the stirrup is reduced and the hearing declines. The condition progresses slowly until the stirrup finally becomes completely fixed and the hearing can then get no worse – at least as far as the conductive element is concerned. Usually one ear is involved first, then, after a delay of several years, the other ear starts to become affected which is when most people begin to notice the problem. Pregnancy is said to speed the process of fixation of the stirrup, so that the hearing deteriorates more quickly during these nine months than during times either side of pregnancy. It has been said that this is the result of very high hormone levels, but there is no good evidence from hearing tests that this is really the case. Furthermore, there is no good evidence that modern oestrogen-containing contraceptive pills or hormone replacement therapy (HRT) has any adverse effects on the progress of otosclerosis

Affected individuals often find that they hear better in the presence of background sound than they do when it is quiet, and this is probably because the background sounds help to get the stirrup moving, and because people talk more loudly when it is noisy. There are several possible ways of managing oto-sclerosis:

- Do nothing. If the condition is not severe enough to cause a problem in day-to-day living, or only one ear is involved, many people do not seek help.

- Wear a hearing aid. Otosclerosis is the condition that is most easily helped by a conventional aid, because all that is needed is to make the incoming sounds loud enough to overcome the obstruction caused by the new bone formation.

- Surgery: it is not possible to remove this new bone growth, but it can be 'bypassed' by removing the arch of the stirrup and drilling a small hole in the footplate so that an artificial bone (prosthesis) can be inserted into the hole in the footplate and connected to the anvil. In effect, the ossicular chain has now been rebuilt in miniature, and is fully mobile so that sound can, once again, be conducted from the eardrum to the inner ear by way of the oval window. Nature has been recreated. This operation is called a stapedectomy (stirrup = stapes and -ectomy = to cut out). More properly it is called a stapedotomy as the stirrup is not removed but a hole is made in it (an -otomy).

When the operation works, the effect is remarkable because the hearing is restored to normal or near normal. However, the major risks of surgery are that changes occur in the inner ear so that the person develops a profound deaf-ness, tinnitus and a balance disturb-ance (vertigo). These are serious, disabling side effects, which can arise without any apparent reason

OTOSCLEROSIS AND STAPEDECTOMY

In otoselerosis the bone surrounding the oval window enlarges reducing the mobility of the stirrup and so hearing declines. This process can be bypassed by an operation called a 'stapedectomy'.

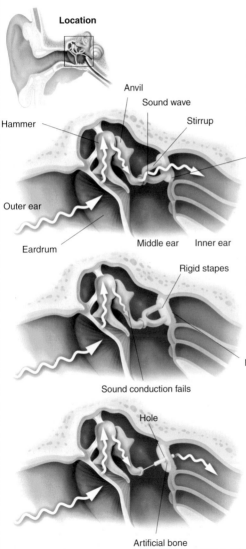

Location

Anvil

Sound wave

Stirrup

Hammer

Oval window

Outer ear

Eardrum

Middle ear   Inner ear

Normal
Sound is transmitted from the eardrum via the three bones of the middle ear which connect to the oval window and the inner ear

Rigid stapes

Sound conduction fails

Bony overgrowth

Otosclerosis
The stapes is immobilised by overgrowth around the base of the stirrup, where it connects to the oval window

Hole

Artificial bone

Surgery for otosclerosis
The arch of the stirrup bone is removed and a small hole is drilled in the footplate so an artificial bone can be inserted. The other end is connected to the anvil, so restoring sound conduction

even in the very best surgical hands. There is an incidence of around one per cent of serious complications, suggesting that it is not the surgical technique that is at fault, but rather the unexpected and unexplained susceptibility of some individuals.

In addition, the nerve that carries taste from the front two-thirds of the tongue – the chorda tympani nerve – also passes through the eardrum on its way to join the facial nerve and thence the brain. This nerve can be damaged or bruised during a stapedectomy, so that the sense of taste on that side alters and people affected frequently complain of a metallic taste. This usually disappears eventually, but it may take many months, and would be a serious complication for anyone who relies on a sense of taste, such as a wine writer or a chef.

Anyone contemplating such an operation must, therefore, be fully aware of these risks before going ahead and must be certain that they cannot cope with hearing aids before subjecting themselves to surgery. Having said this, successful surgery almost always results in a transformation of the individual's life.

MENIÈRE'S DISEASE

Dr Prosper Menière, who was a dedicated and observant Parisian physician, described the symptoms of the condition that now bears his name in 1861. He died in 1862 and is probably turning in his grave at the way his name is used for almost any condition associated with dizziness and perhaps some deafness. Menière's syndrome is classically defined as irregular bouts of sensorineural hearing loss, associated with tinnitus and attacks of vertigo that tend to come in clusters. To these three classic symptoms has been added a fourth – a feeling of pressure in the affected ear.

A typical way for the condition to show itself would be for a young woman who is working hard at her job, often in difficult conditions, to develop a feeling of blockage in one ear and muffled, distorted hearing. She would also experience some tinnitus. These symptoms are often ascribed to a problem with the eustachian tube and treated with decongestants or even with antibiotics. The problem passes only to recur, with possibly a little residual hearing loss, tinnitus and a feeling of a blocked ear. Eventually, and usually within a year of the first onset of symptoms, the woman has an attack of vertigo. This is not a momentary affair, but lasts for many minutes or even hours and can be very distressing. There is usually a short period of increased pressure or worsened hearing or louder tinnitus before the vertigo starts. The surroundings usually appear to spin violently around, although it can be the inside of the head that appears to move. Whether it is the surroundings or the person that appears to move and in whichever direction, it is the sense of unreal movement that is so disturbing and that confirms the symptom of vertigo. Frequently, the vertigo is associated with nausea and vomiting.

Once the vertigo settles, the affected person feels unsteady – maybe for days – and often notices that the hearing has not returned to its previous level, although balance has become normal again.

Attacks come in clusters over several months, and then seem to disappear, often for a year or so, before they recur with a relentless, progressive loss of hearing, and the residual hearing being very distorted.

There are many different forms of the condition, but all four symptoms (blockage, deafness,

Right ear: Menière's disease

An audiogram showing low-tone sensorineural hearing loss, typical of Menière's disease.

tinnitus, vertigo) need to be present for a consultant to make the diagnosis after other conditions – such as middle-ear disease, especially cholesteatoma (see page 53) and acoustic neuromas (see page 68) – have been excluded. Anyone who has symptoms suggestive of Menière's disease should have a full examination and thorough investigations in an ENT clinic to be absolutely certain that this is, in fact, the problem. They can then be strongly reassured that there is nothing more serious or life threatening behind the symptoms.

What causes the problem is not known, but it is more common in people with certain personality types, namely intelligent, well-organised, tidy individuals. This is the same sort of personality who tends to get migraine and indeed there is a strong association within families of Menière's disease and migraine through a genetic, chromosomal linkage. We are not sure of the precise cause of Menière's disease, but presumably the blood supply to the inner ear alters so that the composition of the fluids filling the labyrinth changes; this, in turn, brings about the symptoms and might account for the frequent worsening of problems in women around the time of their periods if there are hormonal changes affecting fluid balance.

If the condition is not treated, recurrent clusters of attacks occur over many years, until it finally 'burns out' to leave hearing loss and tinnitus with normal or near-normal balance. Occasionally, the other ear is affected. The typical pattern of hearing loss is of a low-tone, sensorineural loss, which at first comes and goes, but eventually settles to a fixed level. The high tones are lost with ageing and the person ends up with a 70-dB hearing loss that affects all frequencies equally. It is unusual for the hearing to get a lot worse than this, but the residual hearing is very distorted and may not be very useful.

The balance can be assessed by caloric tests. Here cool and warm water are gently irrigated into each ear in turn. The difference in the water temperature from normal body temperature either stimulates (warm) or inhibits (cool) the balance portion of each ear in turn. This results in a feeling of unreal movement (vertigo) and a rhythmic, oscillating movement of the eyes, called nystagmus, which can be seen if the eyes are observed closely. In Menière's disease, the affected ear may be overactive initially, but soon its function diminishes and this can be detected on the caloric test as a 'paralysis' of the semi-circular canals, which causes less nystagmus.

Treatment is difficult because the cause of Menière's disease is unknown, However, a proper examination, with appropriate investigations and a full explanation of what is thought to be happening, may at least make the person feel less anxious. For anyone who has not experienced a prolonged attack of vertigo, it is difficult to understand how frightening it can be.

People with this condition are advised to reduce their salt and caffeine intake, although complete abstention has not been shown to have any benefit. The only medications that appear to have any beneficial effect on the long-term progress of the attacks of vertigo are thiazide diuretics (water tablets) and betahistine. The acute attack of vertigo can often be helped with short-term medications, such as prochlorperazine and cinnarizine among others. These last two drugs should not, however, be used for long periods because they have side effects, including unsteadiness and clumsiness.

There are various operations that can be performed in an attempt to control the vertigo. The simple insertion of a ventilation tube (grommet) into the eardrum on the affected side helps some people. Operating on the inner ear (a saccus decompression which removes bone covering part of the inner ear – the endolymphatic sac) helps

relieve the vertigo in 70 per cent of individuals for five years or more.

If there is residual hearing, cutting the balance nerve (a vestibular neurectomy) disconnects the misbehaving ear from the brain, although this is a major operation with considerable surgical risks.

If there is no useful hearing and the vertigo is relentless, destroying the inner ear (a labyrinthectomy) will, at worst, replace the vertigo by unsteadiness, which is an acceptable alternative to those who are severely affected.

Treatment of vertigo by the injection of aminoglycoside antibiotics into the middle ear to destroy parts of the middle ear has recently been revived because the newer aminoglycosides have become more predictable in their actions. The aminoglycosides are a group of antibiotics that have the unfortunate side effect of damaging the inner ear. They either damage the inner and outer hair cells of the cochlea, or the hair cells of balance, or both to a greater or lesser degree. These antibiotics are able to get into the inner ear through the membranes of the round and oval windows when injected into the middle ear.

Neomycin almost exclusively damages the cochlea. Gentamicin is much more toxic to the balance portions of the inner ear so it can be used to perform a 'chemical' destruction of the misbehaving balance portion of the inner ear. The procedure is relatively straight-forward and is very effective, although there is always a real risk of seriously damaging the remaining hearing.

At every stage of Menière's disease, there is something that can be done to improve the quality of life of those unfortunate enough to have the disease, although, as the condition progresses, the treatment is more demanding and the emphasis changes from stopping the vertigo to maintaining the hearing.

NOISE-INDUCED HEARING LOSS

Unwanted noise gets everywhere in the Western World. The sound of neighbours' loud parties, road-works, car alarms or the yapping of dogs in the early hours of the morning can all cause an intense irritation to anyone forced to hear these intrusive noises. Hearing is one of our early warning systems and the intrusion of unexpected or unusual sounds puts us on edge, ready to react to possible danger.

Although these sorts of sounds are irritating, they are rarely physically harmful and it is much louder noise that causes damage to the cochlea. With prolonged overload, the outer hair cells (OHCs) simply get exhausted and the internal cochlear amplifier – the

source of otoacoustic emissions – fails. A temporary hearing loss – that is, a threshold shift – develops until the OHCs recover in the relative quiet of a night's sleep. This symptom is often the one noticed first, by those exposed to noise, although they may not appreciate its significance. Newspaper workers in the old days of extremely noisy printing presses sometimes noticed that their cars sounded abnormally noisy on the way to work, but on the way home sounded 'nice and quiet' because their hearing had been affected by the noise of the presses.

This temporary threshold shift (TTS) becomes persistent with continued exposure, so that several months away from noise are necessary for recovery. With continued exposure, a permanent threshold shift (PTS) develops. The frequencies first involved tend to be the higher frequencies, typically those at 4 or 6 kHz, so that a notch appears in the audiogram when a person affected in this way is tested.

Why damage should first appear in this region is not known for sure, but this change on the audiogram in anyone with a history of exposure is almost enough in itself to make a diagnosis of occupational noise-induced hearing loss (ONIHL). If the person continues to be exposed, the notch deepens and broadens and he or she starts to notice a reduction in the ability to hear properly. He or she may have problems hearing in pubs and clubs, and then with hearing the television clearly.

There are several factors that determine who acquires hearing loss as a result of noise. First and probably most significant is the overall noise exposure sustained by the cochlea. This is a combination of the intensity of the sound – that is, the sound energy received by the ear – and the duration of exposure. Doubling the sound energy by increasing the sound level by 3 dB halves the time needed to produce the same damage. Thus, very high sound levels, such as those experienced by gunners in the artillery or from being close to exploding shells, can bring on permanent deafness very quickly in most people.

The second significant factor is individual susceptibility. Virtually no-one sustains hearing loss with environmental sounds below 80 dB, however long the exposure. At 90 dB for an eight-hour working day over a period of years, about 12 per cent of the workforce sustain a typical ONIHL, although the severity varies between individuals. At 85 dB only three per cent sustain damage. At present there is no way of making OHCs regenerate so this loss is permanent.

Noise damage has occurred for years, yet it is only recently that legislation has been enforced to help prevent this avoidable problem. The reasons for the delay are probably a mixture of financial, practical and technical. Making machinery quiet is extremely expensive. Providing hearing protection to reduce the sound energy reaching the ear is relatively easy, but makes communication very difficult, and this can cause problems when there are other, more obvious dangers in the workplace such as moving vehicles and cranes.

Fortunately, with improvements in technology, ear defenders with built-in microphones and radio communication devices are now available, although at some cost. If employers are prepared to provide such devices and enforce their use, then ONIHL should become a disease of the past. Many pop musicians for whom noise damage was an occupational problem now use such devices. Hearing defenders should also be used by the military so that the massive hearing problems caused by gunfire exposure is minimised, even if it cannot be completely prevented.

There are government-backed compensation processes available for people who have been deafened either through exposure in the armed forces or through industrial noise. The criteria for compensation are extremely strict with those for industrial compensation requiring an average 50-dB loss or more at 1, 2 and 3 kHz before an award is made. This is severe deafness, which makes face-to-face conversation in the quiet almost impossible without aids. Similar restrictions apply for those deafened in the service of their country.

Parents frequently ask about the risks faced by their children from headphones and loud popular music. There is definitely a risk at discos, clubs and concerts (especially for those close to speakers) of sustaining noise damage. Most clubbers recognise that they develop tinnitus and muffled hearing after a 'good' night but that this eventually goes away. However, most ENT surgeons continue to see individuals who have sustained a permanent loss that is sometimes profound. This seems to be more likely if they have gone in for energetic dancing and there is some marginal evidence that exercise and oxygen reduction make the cochlea more sensitive to noise. In Paris, several British bands have been forbidden to play in concert because their music was too loud for French standards.

AGE-RELATED HEARING LOSS – PRESBYCUSIS

It is common knowledge that, as the years pass, most people's hearing becomes less acute. The reason for this is that there is a gradual loss of OHCs and to a lesser extent of inner hair cells (IHCs) from the organ of Corti. The loss is worst at the base of the cochlea, which detects the high frequencies that are very important for hearing clearly in background noise but less severe in the middle portions that detect the bulk of the environmental sounds including speech sounds.

The changes in the cochlea seem to start at birth so that there is a gradual loss of hair cells in everyone, although the rate of loss is very different from person to person. There seem to be more hair cells present than are needed for useful hearing. Thus, the effect of this progressive loss is generally not noticed until the person reaches his or her 40s. He or she often starts to find difficulties hearing conversations in background noise (for instance in a restaurant) because the high-frequency loss makes discrimination between voices a problem. Individual voices are typified by a range of particular frequencies called formants and the pattern is distinctive to that voice. To distinguish one voice from another forces the brain to perform a speech pattern analysis and then separate that particular voice from those around it. This requires that the higher formants in the pattern be heard and, if there is a significant high-frequency loss, this simply cannot be done.

Another feature that comes with hair cell loss is called 'recruitment'. Here the hearing levels are reduced so that low sound levels are not detected. Once a detectable volume is reached, there is a rapid growth in the perceived loudness of the sound, which very rapidly becomes unpleasantly loud as the volume is increased. The practical demonstration of recruitment is seen when you enter a room and an elderly relative cannot see you. You say 'hello' in your normal voice and she does not hear you. You raise your voice a little and she still does not hear. You raise your voice again and she turns and retorts: 'Don't shout. I'm not deaf!'

Unfortunately, there is no cure for, or prevention of, age-related hearing loss yet. At present, all that can be done is to make sure the person does not have any treatable ear disease, and provide explanations, environmental aids and the appropriate hearing aids if needed or wanted. Using a hearing aid can be difficult if recruitment is severe, so that aids with some form of electronic control of the maximum output are usually needed for comfort. The hearing aid user needs to get 'acclimatised' to the hearing aid by using it a little at first and gradually increasing usage to allow the ears and brain to accept all the new sounds that were previously unheard.

However, some people are impatient and expect an instant response from a hearing aid and are disappointed when the new sounds from a perfect aid are not those to which they are accustomed. It is important to persevere.

SUDDEN DEAFNESS

The sudden onset of a severe hearing loss is almost always a devastating experience. The effects can be very disturbing even if the loss occurs in only one ear. Sound location, and hearing in background noise, as in restaurants and in difficult acoustic environments such as classrooms, becomes very difficult. Fortunately a profound, sudden loss in both ears is rare. If tinnitus develops the problems are all much worse. A sudden hearing loss can result from many causes but how sudden is sudden and how much of a loss is needed before it can be called a loss?

The usually accepted definition is of a loss of more than 30 dB averaged over three frequencies, and occurring within three days. The causes of such losses are:

• conductive

• sensorineural

- mixture of sensorineural and conductive

- psychological.

Conductive

Although wax is not usually a cause of any significant hearing loss, it can be inadvertently pushed on to the eardrum by a cotton bud, or can swell up when water gets into the ear and cause blockage and hearing loss. This can be removed by careful suction clearance to avoid any trauma that can occur with syringing.

Acute changes that are not enough to damage the eardrum and that can occur during scuba diving or on flying with a cold can result in bleeding into the middle ear or just outpouring of fluid from the lining of the middle ear. The fluid can be removed by making an incision in the eardrum (called a myringotomy) and applying careful suction through the incision.

Severe sudden conductive losses usually come from trauma to the eardrum or middle ear. This can be caused by a diving injury or blast exposure when the eardrum is extensively damaged. This is often obvious from the history of events and a simple examination, which shows the ruptured eardrum. A maximum 40-dB loss can occur with this type of damage.

Direct head trauma such as might occur in a car crash can disrupt the ossicular chain. The most common site of damage is the joint between the anvil and stirrup (the incudo-stapedial joint). When this occurs there is complete discontinuity and a 60-dB conductive loss.

In all the above cases, reliable pure-tone audiometry with masked bone conduction must be performed to exclude an underlying sensorineural hearing loss caused by the trauma, which would alter the chances of full recovery. Tympanometry, when the eardrum is intact, may show a tall, peaked wave typical of ossicular discontinuity or a flat trace if the middle ear is full of fluid

Ossicular problems can frequently be cured by surgery. The eardrum is reconnected to the stirrup using either the patient's own anvil (that has been reshaped and re-inserted between the handle of the hammer and the stirrup) or artificial bone. This is commonly made of hydroxyapatite, one of the core elements of bone. The procedure is called an ossiculoplasty. The eardrum can also be repaired again using microsurgical techniques and the procedure is called a tympanoplasty or myringoplasty.

Sensorineural

Severe acute sensorineural hearing losses (SNHLs) are not particularly common and most general practitioners will not see more than a handful in their lifetimes. This has made evaluation of the best forms of treatment very difficult. A few people have a specific causative condition such as blast injury or major pressure damage, which has traumatised the cochlea. Others will have had meningitis or mumps. Severe middle-ear infections or cholesteatoma can invade the inner ear. An acoustic neuroma (described later) can also make itself known by producing a sudden deafness. A few people will have had a herpes infection and, in addition to some blisters in the ear or on the roof of the mouth, might have vertigo and a facial palsy (see page 7) as well as the deafness. This collection of symptoms is called the Ramsay Hunt syndrome.

There are other rarer conditions, but in general there is no proven cause for most cases of sudden onset SNHLs. When this happens, doctors tend to label the condition as being caused by a virus or a blood clot affecting the blood supply to the inner ear. There is no good evidence to support either of these causes as being 'real', although the second has more substance. The inner ear has only a single small artery (the labyrinthine artery) supplying it whereas most other parts of the body have two, so that if one is blocked the other continues the supply. The labyrinthine artery divides to supply the cochlea and the vestibular labyrinth separately. Blockage of the artery at various points could theoretically cause deafness, dizziness or both. Although this is an attractive proposition and has formed the basis for many treatments, there is no proof that this is the cause. For this reason most cases of acute SNHLs are called idiopathic, which means without cause.

Thus, for a condition without a cause, treatment cannot be planned on any logical basis. Indeed, in proper trials no form of treatment has been shown to be any more effective than doing nothing – provided other underlying conditions have been excluded. Untreated, 60 to 70 per cent of individuals recover completely or almost completely and usually within the first week. The factors that suggest poor recovery are:

- losses involving the 8-kHz region

- a loss averaging more than 70 dB at 1, 2 and 4 kHz

- associated vertigo.

However, this is not to say that patients do not need to be treated. A sudden-onset severe loss is a seriously debilitating condition because hearing is one of the body's early warning systems and losing it causes great internal anxiety and distress. Any residual hearing is usually distorted and unpleasant recruitment is common. If tinnitus develops this makes the problem worse. A full history should be taken, an examination performed and appropriate investigations ordered to exclude underlying disease. Many ENT surgeons like to admit their patients for bed rest and sedation, and possibly medication because of the disturbing nature of the problem. Should recovery not occur, support and hearing rehabilitation can be provided.

Psychological

During depressive illnesses a few people develop what has been called a conversion reaction, when their disorder shows itself as a specific physical complaint. A common change is an acute but severe memory loss or an acute blindness. Less commonly, a severe deafness can occur. This can also be part of a traumatic stress disorder, especially if a blast or explosion has occurred and there has been a 'real' but temporary reduction in the hearing. These cases are often difficult to manage. The individual frequently produces a flat audiogram at around 50 to 70 dB, which would be very unusual in the vast majority of conditions with middle- or inner-ear disease. Fortunately, testing for otoacoustic emissions or auditory evoked potentials can give the true hearing levels, which is both an aid to diagnosis and a help in management because at least the patient can be reassured that the hearing will get better and appropriate treatments put in place.

ACOUSTIC NEUROMAS

Although acoustic neuromas are not common, they can cause serious or even life-threatening problems whether they are left alone or treated. This is slightly peculiar because they are absolutely benign, non-cancerous growths, arising from the cells that surround and insulate the balance nerves. These cells are called the Schwann cells and the balance nerve is the vestibular nerve, so that technically the correct name for these growths is 'vestibular schwannomas'; this name is often used in medical literature.

They occur quite commonly but only rarely result in symptoms; they affect about one in 100,000 of the population each year, so that doctors in England and Wales see approximately 400 new cases of acoustic neuromas each year. The symptoms and the serious nature of the condition arise from the location of the growths and the important structures that lie nearby.

As the hearing and balance nerves leave the inner ear, they pass inwards through a narrow canal in the skull called the internal auditory meatus (IAM). There is then a gap between the inner surface of the skull and the brain called the cerebellopontine angle (CPA). This space is filled with the fluid that bathes the brain (the cerebrospinal fluid or CSF). The two nerves cross this space, joining together as they do so, and enter the brain stem. The brain stem controls many vital functions such as breathing, blood pressure, pulse, balance, eye movements and many of the unconscious activities that we take for granted. Also arising from this region are the nerves that control swallowing, speech, chewing and facial sensation. One very important nerve in this region is the facial nerve. This arises close to the entry of the hearing and balance nerves, and travels out with these two nerves into the IAM along to the end of the canal. Then, in a complicated path, the facial nerve runs through the middle ear and mastoid bone to end up supplying all the muscles of facial expression – that is, smiling, flaring of the nostrils, closing the eyes and wrinkling the forehead.

As acoustic neuromas start to grow, they begin to compress the structures around them and interfere with their function, eventually causing symptoms. If the growths start within the IAM, one-sided tinnitus, distorted hearing and hearing loss may occur. Loss of balance is not often a problem. If the growths start further in, they can remain 'silent' for a long while until the brain stem starts to be compressed, when clumsiness, facial numbness or pains, or slurred speech develops. Eventually, the pressure on the brain stem restricts the flow of cerebrospinal fluid and the pressure in the head starts to rise. This causes nausea, vomiting, headaches, fevers, increased clumsiness, blurred vision and reduced consciousness, possibly leading to seizures and death.

Acoustic neuromas grow slowly, on average one to two millimetres each year, but there is not a lot of space inside the base of the skull and most tumours need treatment. It is obvious from what has been said above that removal is not going to be easy, and in general the larger the tumour the greater the risks of surgery. The surgeon's aim is to remove the acoustic neuroma completely without causing any additional damage to surrounding nerves or to the brain. The nerve most at risk is the facial nerve because this gets stretched around the tumour mass and so can become extremely thin and fragile. Despite advances in surgical technique, facial nerve monitoring and anaesthesia, preservation of a stretched facial nerve requires considerable skill, although damage can occur even in the best surgical hands.

Non-surgical treatment is with concentrated radiotherapy – so-called stereotactic radiotherapy. The aim is to prevent further growth of the tumour. Although this technique has been in use for some years now, its value has still to be fully evaluated and indeed surgery after radiotherapy, should the treatment fail to stop the tumour growing, presents a major challenge to the surgeon because the scarring around the tumour makes it virtually impossible to preserve the facial nerve. Stereotactic radiotherapy can be given in multiple small doses when it is called fractionated stereotactic radiotherapy (FSRT) or in one big dose when it is called gamma knife treatment. There is some evidence that FSRT is gentler to surrounding tissues than the gamma knife.

In general, one-sided auditory symptoms need to be investigated thoroughly and magnetic resonance imaging gives a safe and absolutely precise diagnosis of these particular tumours. There is, therefore, no reason not to have the investigation, although there is usually no great urgency unless there are major symptoms suggesting that a large tumour is present or that there is raised pressure inside the skull.

KEY POINTS

✓ There are many causes of a hearing loss; only a few have been described

✓ Most of these causes are not serious and can easily be remedied

✓ If you think that your hearing is deteriorating, especially if it is in one ear and there are other symptoms such as tinnitus, you should seek advice

✓ Conductive hearing losses can often be helped by surgery, although sensorineural losses cannot; all losses can be helped with the appropriate aids

Hearing loss in the UK

The term 'deafness' has many connotations and although one individual may not consider himself deaf, the rest of his family may be at their wits' end because of an overloud television or a failure to hear the doorbell or telephone.

Some more precise terminology is required not only to be able to assess the extent of the problem but also to allow appropriate resources to be allocated to those groups most in need. The terms 'hearing impairment', 'disability' and 'handicap' have been used for many years to help provide a sensible framework for discussions between those groups with deaf interests at heart and the various government agencies. These terms are under review at present because they may be thought to be politically incorrect.

HEARING IMPAIRMENT

Hearing impairment is a number in decibels obtained from a measurement known as the pure-tone audiogram (see page 26). It is calculated for each ear as the average hearing level for several different frequencies. For many purposes, industrial deafness claims or war pension claims, for example, the hearing levels in decibels at one, two and three kilohertz (1, 2 and 3 kHz) are averaged. This measure tends to underestimate both the severity of the hearing loss because noise damage tends to involve the higher frequencies (that is, 4 and 6 kHz first), and the impact of the loss on hearing in background noise, which is the major complaint of most claimants.

The measure used by the Medical Research Council's (MRC's) Institute of Hearing Research (IHR), in their national survey of hearing completed in 1989, was the average at 0.5, 1, 2 and 4 kHz. The MRC felt that this was a more appropriate indicator because it gave a better prediction of the problems besetting normal people.

DISABILITY

Disability is the overall difficulty that a hearing impairment causes an individual in his or her daily life. Examples are specific, such as being unable to hear properly in background noise; finding the television and radio difficult to understand; and not hearing the door bell, the telephone or the 'ping' on the microwave oven that tells you that something is cooked. Disability can be rated on a scale of 0 to 100 per cent.

HANDICAP

Handicap is the effect that this disability has on an individual's overall quality of life. An individual may become socially withdrawn because of difficulties in conversation and not wanting to be thought stupid. There can be major problems with education, employment, within the family and with all interpersonal relationships. Handicap is a complex outcome and depends on the personality of the deaf individual, the support of those close by and the social environment. At one extreme, a monk living in a monastery retreat may be profoundly deaf with an almost 100 per cent disability yet have no handicap whatsoever. Indeed the absence of distractions by outside sounds may be a positive benefit to his meditations. Was deafness a handicap to Beethoven's musical output? Most individuals are, however, deeply distressed by the onset of more severe forms of hearing loss and deafness causes them a major handicap in their lives. Everything changes for them and their families.

In 1989 the Census office looked at the various self-reported disabilities across the nation. Although 'mobility problems' were the most common, 'hearing difficulties' were the second most common disability, affecting seven million of the population.

The IHR undertook a national study of hearing. Some 50,000 questionnaires were sent asking people for their assessment of their own hearing, tinnitus and the use of the NHS for assistance. It was found that young people tended to overrate their hearing disability whereas elderly people consistently underrated it. Thus, an extensive audiometric survey was performed to assess the prevalence – that is, the total number of affected people in the population at any one time – of the severity and different types of hearing loss. The hearing impairment in the better hearing ear was used as a predictor because it was felt that this was a better indicator of the overall disability.

The extent of the problem is difficult to comprehend. Sixteen per cent of the adult population had average hearing at 0.5, 1, 2 and 4 kHz of 25 dB or worse in the better ear. Nearly 90 per cent of these losses were sensorineural in origin. As the losses get more severe there is an increase in the number with a conductive element to the loss. The data also showed that young people had relatively few problems as a group, but that, once past the age of 50, the prevalence increased rapidly indicating that most deafness is acquired. One in three of the total number with hearing impairment was over the age of 80.

Thus, about one in seven of the population has some problem – hence the title of the excellent house magazine of the Royal National Institute for Deaf People (*One in seven*). These figures are probably applicable to most Westernised societies and include those who are born with a severe hearing impairment. The general figures are that about 1 in a 1,000 children is born with hearing levels worse than 50 dB and that each year another 3 people in every 10,000 becomes severely deafened, usually as a result of meningitis.

Overall, the figures show that there is a massive core of disability that requires a huge resource in financial terms for aids for hearing-impaired individuals, in commitment to equal opportunities and in human involvement in minimising handicap.

THE PREVALENCE OF HEARING LOSS IN THE UK

Severity of hearing loss in decibels in better ear	Classification	Prevalence in population	Numbers in the UK
25 dB or worse	Mild	16.1%	7.6 million
45 dB or worse	Moderate	4.9%	2.3 million
65 dB or worse	Severe	1%	0.5 million
85 dB or worse	Profound	0.4%	About 200,000

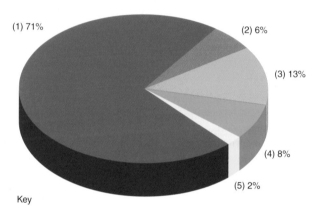

THE APPROXIMATE PREVALENCE OF DIFFERENT HEARING IMPAIRMENT TYPES IN THE UK POPULATION

(1) 71%

(2) 6%

(3) 13%

(4) 8%

(5) 2%

Key

(1) Normal hearing

(2) Sensorineural loss in one ear

(3) Sensorineural loss in both ears

(4) Conductive loss in one ear

(5) Conductive loss in both ears

KEY POINTS

✓ One in seven of the UK population have some hearing loss

✓ The major cause of hearing loss is a sensorineural loss in both ears

✓ Once past the age of 50, the problem becomes more common

✓ There is a massive amount of disability and handicap from deafness

Aids to hearing

From the previous chapters, it has become clear that most causes of deafness are sensorineural (involving the inner ear, auditory pathway and brain) in origin and only relatively few are conductive. At present there is no specific cure or indeed any medical treatment for the vast majority of sensorineural losses.

It is the conductive losses that can often be treated with surgery to repair and reconstruct damaged or diseased parts of the outer and middle ears. Some of these conditions and their treatments have been described in preceding chapters. Ironically, it is the conductive losses that are also most easily managed by hearing aids because the inner ear is usually intact. All the hearing aid has to do is increase the volume of sound to overcome the conductive 'block'. In sensorineural losses, the loss of hair cells and auditory nerve fibres reduces the quality of the information going to the brain, so that, however good the aid, it is limited by the quality of the information that can be passed on to the brain.

Aids to hearing come in a wide variety of forms and this chapter tries to outline what is available. Hearing therapists within the NHS are trained to give appropriate advice and provide help wherever possible and within the constraints of a rather small budget. A special service called LINK is provided for those with severe problems, but people must be referred to it by an NHS consultant. LINK has been of enormous assistance to many, but its funding is not assured, although in the author's personal view, and with respect to the many grateful patients, it should be.

SIGN LANGUAGE

For those born deaf, especially into families where the parents are deaf, 'signing' is a truly marvellous form of communication and there are virtually no barriers to what can be achieved. The major obstacle to its use is that hearing people tend to treat this part of the deaf community as if they have a disease – which of course they do not. The deaf community generally distrust doctors and the like who try to 'cure' them of their hearing loss when they, the deaf community, rightly, do not accept that hearing loss, in itself, is a handicap. It is society in general that is intolerant and society should be more accepting.

The other barrier is that there is not yet an internationally accepted sign language, which is a problem. There is a fairly uniform British sign language that takes time to learn but, with effort, fluency can be achieved, and the more 'hearers' who can learn sign language, the quicker the communication barriers between people with and without hearing can be broken down. The information in Useful addresses includes details of how to find out more about signing.

LIP-READING

For people who acquire deafness, even quite profound deafness, lip-reading skills may be the only means they have available to overcome their difficulties in face-to-face communication. Understanding the spoken language is a very high-level skill. It requires the ears to hear the various major elements of speech, the eyes to read the lips and assess facial expression and body posture, and the brain to analyse the context of what is being said and to make sense of all the incoming information in the light of experience. The ability to hear speech is only one part, albeit a large part, of communication.

We must all have played the game of Chinese whispers where a secret message is whispered from one person to the next. Being a whisper, this will often be misheard; you cannot lip-read and you don't know the context. Normally, you would ask for the words to be repeated if you could not quite make sense of what was being said. However, the rules of the game insist that you make a decision as to what you think you heard and the message that comes out at the end of the chain is usually quite wrong and often very amusing.

The most common reason for poor communication is reduced hearing and enhancing the lip-reading abilities of those who have developed deafness may be very useful. There are definite strategies than can enable you to become a better lip-reader and most local education authorities run classes to teach them.

ENVIRONMENTAL AIDS

As electronic technology becomes increasingly sophisticated, a wide range of devices is being devised to help individuals cope with day-to-day life. In the early days, the options were simple: to increase the volume or to alter the tone of the sound in question so that it stood out from the background sounds. The doorbell could be made louder, extension bells might be placed around the house or the tone of the bell could be made low pitched – as most forms of hearing loss have relatively well-preserved low tones.

The same modifications can be made to baby alarms and fire alarms, and all can have flashing lights incorporated somewhere sensible. For all alarm systems, even for alarm clocks, vibrators buried within pillows for use at night can be incorporated into the system to make it almost foolproof. Telephones can be amplified and televisions can have suitable personal amplifiers either directly wired or radio-transmitted to the individual listener.

Most hearing aids have facilities for detecting the electromagnetic waves that are produced from loudspeakers or from 'loop' systems. In these, a wire is run around the outside of the room or hall and attached to an amplifier, which is in turn connected to an appropriately placed microphone or to the sound output of a television, radio or other device. The hearing aid has a switch (usually marked 'T') and, when this is on, the aid detects the signal from the loop without the background noise. This can be an absolute boon in meetings, at theatres and in church, although there are occasional interesting moments when the vicar inadvertently forgets to turn off his microphone and those using the loop system can hear his comments although the rest of the congregation cannot.

Until recently, it was not possible to provide a text or signed translation of what was being said on the telephone, television or radio, but there has been much progress in this area of late. There is Teletext on the television and Minicom telephones. Some television programmes can be broadcast with split screens, with a signer providing simultaneous translation. With the advent of digital radio, it should be possible to add a visual text bar to the set much as Teletext is added to the television.

All NHS hearing aid centres should be able to provide information about how to obtain and install the relevant environmental aids and the RNID also offers comprehensive guidance.

CONVENTIONAL HEARING AIDS

Conventional hearing aids are available either through the NHS or privately. At present the provision of an NHS aid generally requires an initial referral by the general practitioner to the local ENT department, where a doctor first excludes treatable diseases that could be causing the hearing loss. The individual is then transferred to the hearing aid centre. In some regions, direct referral to the hearing aid centre attached to the ENT unit is possible. Here the audiologists and hearing therapists undertake the screening and, if they find problems, send the individual on to the ENT surgeon.

Hearing aids can be bought privately and are generally quite expensive, although the aids are now much more robust than they used to be and should last for eight to ten years. They can be provided only by people who have passed the Hearing Aid Council examinations so that quality control should be in place. There should be a trial period of four to six weeks, after which the aid can be returned with only administrative costs. If this option is not offered then go elsewhere.

Acoustic aids

A conventional hearing aid consists of a microphone, an amplifier requiring a source of power and a loudspeaker. Since the introduction, in the 1950s, of the rather large and cumbersome Medical Research Council aids for the NHS, there have been major developments in battery technology and electronics, which have allowed the aids to become smaller and more effective.

At present mild-to-moderate hearing losses can be helped with small aids that sit within the ear canal and in the shell-like portion of the pinna – the concha. There are smaller aids called IC (in-the-canal) aids, which are more or less hidden within the ear canal, but there is a limit to their power at present because of their size. Aids that are totally within the canal are being developed.

Very severe losses need more power and in general need a larger aid than can be fitted in the canal and concha. This type of aid (called a BE aid) therefore sits behind the ear and a small tube carries the sound into a mould or shell that fits into the ear canal. A very few people will need an aid with still more power than a BE aid can produce and this can be provided with a body-worn (BW) aid, which can be carried, for example, in a top pocket. The aid is connected by a wire to the ear mould, which houses the small loudspeaker.

The processing of the incoming sound by the amplifier has also

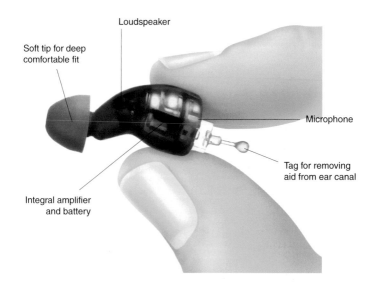

Soft tip for deep
comfortable fit

Loudspeaker

Microphone

Tag for removing
aid from ear canal

Integral amplifier
and battery

IC (in-the-canal) hearing aids fit largely within the ear canal, but there is a limit to their power at present.

undergone enormous changes. Many hearing losses such as those that arise from ageing or noise damage are restricted to the higher frequencies. This sort of loss with relatively normal mid- and low-tone hearing would be difficult to overcome if the amplifier simply magnified all sound frequencies. The result would be that the low tones, which are often general environmental noises such as traffic, air conditioning, etc., would become unbearable.

One way out of this is to make a ventilation hole in the ear mould itself, which reduces the volume of the low tones at the eardrum.

However, this can introduce 'feedback' which is a high-pitched whine as amplified sound from the loudspeaker escapes from the ear canal via the vent, is detected by the microphone of the hearing aid and amplified, and again escapes only to enter an endless loop. This 'feedback' sound also occurs when hearing aid moulds do not fit properly and is often a source of severe irritation to the family and friends of the person wearing the hearing aid. This can easily be remedied by having a well-fitting mould made.

An alternative is to use electronics so that the high frequencies are let through and amplified by high-pass filters (filters that let through the high frequencies). Recently, the introduction of digital signal processing – the basis of CD technology – has made it possible to produce digital hearing aids. In digital signal processing, signals are broken down into very short segments, each being given a numerical value that can then be processed. Many people who have moved to digital aids say that, although these aids are not perfect, they are a lot better than the earlier analogue aids. There are no scientific studies to confirm this yet. At present digital aids are more expensive than conventional, analogue aids.

An amplifier may also make sounds too loud for comfort. This is especially a problem for people with a cochlear type of sensorineural hearing loss in which recruitment occurs. For these people there is only a small volume change between the level of sound that they can just hear and that which is uncomfortable. Before a hearing aid can be fitted, the loudness discomfort levels at each pitch should be measured and the output of the aid adjusted accordingly. This is possible with conventional aids but much easier for a digital aid, which can usually be pre-set or programmed with the individual user's audiogram and discomfort levels to ensure

comfortable listening levels.

Amplifiers are now available that reproduce the incoming signal perfectly. They can be tuned or programmed to give an output that matches the pattern of the audiogram, so that only the involved frequencies are made louder. Yet many people who wear hearing aids still complain that they cannot hear speech in background noise or that picking out one voice in a crowd is impossible. One part of the problem is that the performance of all hearing aids falls away in the frequencies above 4 kHz, which are those needed for performing difficult auditory tasks such as hearing individual voices in background noise. However, even if perfect aids could be made, a greater problem still exists: as the outer and then the inner hair cells are lost, there is an eventual loss of auditory nerve fibres. When this happens, there is simply not enough information reaching the person's brain to enable them to hear speech in difficult background noise. The hearing is still good enough to hear warning sounds, but it cannot provide the very high-level information that is needed for understanding speech.

Many people are disappointed when they first wear a hearing aid because the sounds are 'tinny' and not what they expect. They want an aid to restore perfect hearing in the

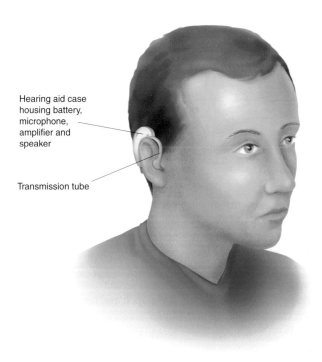

Hearing aid case housing battery, microphone, amplifier and speaker

Transmission tube

BE (behind-the-ear) hearing aids are used for more severe hearing losses. The battery, microphone, amplifier and speaker sit in a case behind the ear. Amplified sound is piped to the ear canal via a tube.

same way that a good pair of glasses restores near-perfect vision for people with many types of visual loss. However, hearing is a complex skill and, despite the fact that an aid suddenly restores sounds that have not been heard for many years, it still takes time for the brain to acclimatise. Once it has done so, the sounds become clearer. It is generally accepted that this acclimatisation can take up to three months; when you first start to use a hearing aid, you should increase the length of time you wear it a little each day until, eventually, you are wearing it for most of the day. Once you have acclimatised then you can wear the aid when needed.

Bone-conducting aids

Sound energy can be transferred by means of a vibrator to the inner ear by direct passage through the skull. This is called bone conduction and can form the basis of a very useful form of hearing aid, although it relies on having good inner-ear function on at least one side. There is, however, a limit to the usefulness of bone-conducting aids because the power output and energy transfer of the vibrator are not as great as with a conventional acoustic aid. A bone-conducting aid will not help someone with significant sensorineural hearing loss, but can be extremely useful for people with a significant conductive deafness in both ears. This might include those who have a discharging wet ear, perhaps as a result of a perforated eardrum, or some other problem such as a sensitivity to the materials of a conventional hearing aid mould or inflammation of the skin of the ear canal caused by eczema.

The simplest version of the bone conductor comprises a sprung metallic band that goes across the head with a small microphone, amplifier and vibrator contained in a unit at one end of the band, which presses against the mastoid bone. Some degree of pressure is needed to achieve good sound conduction and some people find this uncomfortable at first. Such an arrangement is a good temporary measure after middle-ear and mastoid surgery, when there is a conductive loss in both ears. Some hearing has to be provided as the operated ear is usually full of antiseptic packing material and there is still the conductive loss on the unoperated

side. (It is usual only to perform major surgery on one ear at a time.)

Wearing a hair band all the time may just be acceptable for a woman, but for a man who cannot conceal it under his hair, this type of aid is not usually a reasonable solution. Fortunately, the bone-conducting aids can be fitted into the frames of spectacles with the curved portion that goes behind the ear incorporating the electronics and the battery, making the aid relatively invisible. The microphones can be hidden in the surrounds of the lenses.

Bone-anchored hearing aids
The bone-conducting aids described above work well but, if it is likely that they will be needed on a long-term basis, an alternative is a bone-anchored aid. A titanium screw is fitted into a carefully threaded hole that has been drilled in the skull behind the ear, usually at the hairline. The skin surrounding the screw is thinned right down or else removed and grafted with a very thin skin graft so that there is not a big bulge of skin around the device. The titanium is then allowed to integrate with the bone over a six-week period, after which the vibrator can be attached to the screw with a specially designed intermediary piece.

Before such an aid can be fitted, it is necessary to ascertain that the person has good inner-ear function. This means that trials with conventional bone-conduction devices must have shown good results so that a successful outcome from surgery can be predicted. The skin around the titanium screw needs continued care, because there is a 'foreign body' in the scalp and this has to be kept clean to avoid infection. The aid may be rather conspicuous if the wearer has short hair.

Despite all these constraints, bone-anchored aids have provided a remarkable improvement in the quality of life for many people because they have both restored hearing and often allowed wet, unpleasant ears to dry out.

Bone-anchored hearing aids are available through the NHS, although not all ENT units are able to provide the service because a skilled team is necessary for the assessment, surgery and follow-up.

IMPLANTABLE AIDS

Recently, there has been a fashion for designing very small vibrators, which can be fixed by special glues or by fine wire clips on to the malleus or anvil in the middle ear. The vibrators are small crystals that change shape when electricity is applied to them. (This so-called piezo-electric effect is used in reverse in some gas lighters where pressure on the crystal generates a spark.) In the ear the electricity to vibrate the crystal comes from the amplifier of a hearing aid, so that the crystal vibrates 'in tune' with the sound; this vibration is passed on to the inner ear by the ossicles. Some research groups feel that this would give better sound quality than is possible by conventional aids.

There still has to be an external microphone and the resulting electrical signal still has to be transferred across the skin to the underlying amplifier and electrical output device. The long-term effects of having a vibrating weight glued or clipped to the ossicles has not been evaluated and, once again, there has to be relatively good inner-ear function with losses no greater than 50 or 60 dB and a normal middle ear. A recent development has been to have the microphone implanted into the walls of the ear canal so that the whole device is buried. The batteries, which are buried under the skin in either of these two types of device, are rechargeable using a radiofrequency energy transmitter. The applications of technology are amazing. Although surgeons are very keen on these devices because they test their surgical skills, it is not at all clear that these aids offer any hearing benefit over a modern digital acoustic aid and certainly there is a surgical risk. At present implantable aids are experimental and are not generally available

CLEVER TRICKS

People who have complete hearing loss in one ear can experience a major problem in terms of hearing in groups, especially at meetings or around a meal table where speakers can be sitting on the individual's deaf side. The devices that help this are CROS aids. This stands for contralateral routing of signal and means that the sounds from the deaf side are picked up by a microphone and the signal is taken round to the better hearing ear, amplified if necessary and then presented to that ear.

This can be achieved by having the transfer wires hidden in spectacle frames, by thin wires running in the hair behind the head or even by radio-transfer from small receivers/transmitters in the deaf ear, with a receiver/loudspeaker in the good ear. With time, the brain starts to recognise the difference between the direct input and the re-routed signal, so that the ability to localise sound can also return. Many people find that this has revolutionised their lives as far as meetings and group occasions are concerned. Some of these CROS systems are available through the NHS although the patient might have to be very persistent to gain access to the service. In some parts of the country, however, there is not the funding available locally to provide the service.

ELECTRONIC AIDS: COCHLEAR IMPLANTS

When the inner ear is severely damaged, conventional aids cannot help because there are simply not enough hair cells remaining to generate sufficient signal to make sense of language. In the past, individuals in this situation were consigned to a life of near silence, relying on lip-reading or signing for communication. For those who acquired a profound loss in adult life, the transition to a silent world was usually extremely depressing and some became suicidal.

For children born profoundly deaf, their silent world was not such a problem, but even with the best will in the world those children rarely, if ever, acquired speech that could be understood by anyone but their parents.

Each year in the UK, out of the 800,000 births, there are about 150 children born profoundly deaf and about another 80 who become so after having meningitis. Fortunately, this second figure should decline as more vaccines are developed against bacterial meningitis and parents become more aware of the dangers.

Hair cells are needed to convert sound to electrical impulses and to start the process of hearing. It is not yet possible to replace missing or dead cochlear hair cells, but if there are still acoustic nerve fibres left these can be used to carry any electrical impulses that can be delivered to them. This job can be carried out by electronic rather than acoustic aids.

The system still comprises a microphone and amplifier linked to a signal processor, but instead of a sound output it produces an electrical output that is related to the pattern (waveform) of the original sound. Early attempts to do this involved the use of single electrodes placed on the round window membrane. This showed that the idea could work and subsequent developments resulted in multiple electrodes embedded in a fine flexible strip which could be threaded into the cochlea by way of a small drill hole (cochleostomy) made near the round window.

This electrode coils around the central core of the cochlea and lies very close to the remaining acoustic nerve fibres. A signal processor with a magnet in it is buried in a recess drilled in the skull under the scalp behind and above the external ear. A radiofrequency transmitter with a magnet in it is on the outside and is held to the skin overlying the processor by magnetic attraction. A microphone collects sound and converts it to an electrical signal, which is then transferred across the skin along with a power supply by the transmitter to a receiver in the signal processor. This then generates the electrical impulse that travels to the electrode buried in the cochlea.

There are many different makes of electrode and several different speech-processing strategies in use today. These are all trying to get the best 'hearing' response for the individual user. For those in whom the device works well, the effects are miraculous and some patients can even use a conventional telephone.

Adults can have such a device implanted at any time, but babies born deaf and those becoming deaf before they can talk (prelingually deafened) should be implanted as soon as possible and certainly before the age of three or four years. If this is not done their speech will never develop. If implantation is delayed past the age of four, the results are very disappointing because the auditory pathways in the brain fail to develop in the absence of stimulation and, after a while, shut down, so that the child never acquires speech of any quality.

This makes it very important to screen all babies using OAE (otoacoustic emission testing – see page 36). Any babies with profound losses can be detected early, and the difficult decisions about whether to implant can be made without undue hurry. Unfortunately, this screening is not yet done in the UK because of the high cost implications

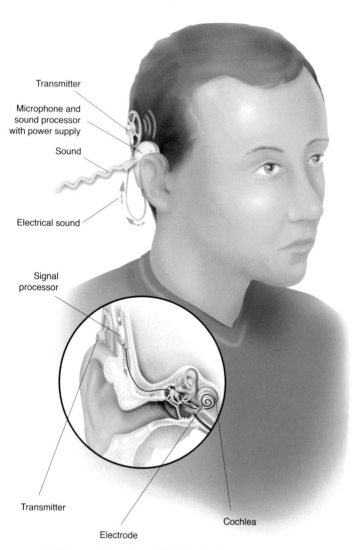

Transmitter

Microphone and
sound processor
with power supply

Sound

Electrical sound

Signal
processor

Transmitter

Electrode

Cochlea

A cochlear implant can be used to deliver electrical stimulation to the acoustic
nerve fibres in the cochlea. The system still comprises a microphone and amplifier,
but instead of a sound output an electrical output is produced that is relayed directly
into the cochlea. More recent developments include an ear-level sound processor so
that the system has no wires.

of detecting deafness.

Children who are born hearing and become deaf (usually through meningitis) after they have learnt to talk can also be helped by a cochlear implant. The sooner it can be performed the less time is lost from education and general social development.

Cochlear implants and bone-anchored hearing aids are provided by the NHS, provided local funding can be obtained. The aids themselves are expensive, for example, the cochlear implant device itself costs about £12,000 and requires a skilled team to ensure that the best implant type is chosen, fitted and tuned. Most health authorities will support the cost of cochlear implants in children and babies because of the adverse publicity and public outcry if they refuse funding. This is not the same for adults and several health authorities refuse to fund implants for those profoundly deaf people who would be likely to benefit!

KEY POINTS

✓ Whatever the problem, there is some form of hearing aid that will help

✓ Aids can be acoustic, bone conducting or electronic

✓ Modern technologies are improving the quality of aids

✓ Hearing aids, at present, will be limited by how much information reaches the brain if the auditory nerve is deficient or damaged

✓ Advances in technology and promising developments in regeneration in the inner ear hold great hopes for the future

Tinnitus

Tinnitus is the term used to describe a condition in which the person 'hears' sounds that are the result of changes in the auditory pathway not triggered by 'genuine' sounds arising in the world outside their head. The sounds certainly seem real enough and someone with tinnitus can spend hours or days looking for leaking pipes or poor electrical connections to explain the hissing or buzzing noises that suddenly develop, often heard for the first time at night when all else is quiet. Tinnitus can in turn bring on great psychological stresses, which seems strange at first sight because tinnitus is only 'sound' after all.

This chapter tries to explain why tinnitus can be so distressing, what causes it and how it can be managed.

WHY TINNITUS IS SO DISTRESSING

Animals have hearing as an early warning system as a first line of defence for survival, and which puts them on 'alert' (see box opposite). In humans, as well as the basic inbuilt 'animal' responses, we also have 'thoughts, feelings and emotions' piled on top and interacting with each other.

There is a short time between the detection of sound by the cochlea and the perception of sound by the auditory cortex in the brain. Nevertheless, in this short period all sorts of interactions can occur. A quarter of a second is a long time for a fast computer and also for our brains.

Not only do we hear sound but we can also be affected by it both physically and emotionally in many ways.

There cannot be any one of us who has not felt that pleasant, exciting tingle down the spine when listening to a particularly enchanting passage of music.

We do not know all that much about the interactions and connections between the auditory pathway and other parts of the brain. How they work is even less well understood. Suffice it to say that unusual electrical activity in the auditory pathway, anywhere from the cochlea to close to the auditory cortex, can have many and varied effects.

Changes in electrical activity in the auditory pathway, for whatever reason, are perceived by the brain as 'sound', even though no new sound may be present in the environment. The auditory cortex does not 'know' that this new activity is not external; it simply recreates it as sound. Likewise, the brain stem does not 'know' that the new electrical activity is not an external threat; it just responds as if it were.

Compare this to what would happen if I were to poke you in the eye: apart from the pain, you would

THE EARLY WARNING EFFECT

- For animals in the wild, an unexpected sound, such as the rustle of leaves or the hiss of moving grass, brings an early warning of possible danger, perhaps a snake. During this time, the brain stem is active, preparing the animal for the worst. The animal's heart rate increases, its pulse quickens, its breathing becomes deeper and quicker, and it pumps out adrenaline.

- The animal is on edge, ready to flee or fight if the source of the sound turns out to be an enemy. The state of alertness continues until the animal determines that the sound was only wind rustling the leaves or running through the tall grass. The state of alertness then settles and the animal's brain stem returns to 'stand by'.

- Skilled producers of horror movies use this effect to get their audiences on the edge of their seats by moving into darkness and then introducing peculiar sounds from different directions. The audience's adrenaline starts to flow and they grip the arms of their seats. Many people know from experience that creaky noises heard in a darkened house at night bring about the sensations of fear and anxiety.

almost certainly 'see' a flash of light. I have not flashed a light in your eye, but the altered electrical activity in the visual system is perceived by your visual cortex as 'light'. In classic migraine, where the blood supply to the visual cortex is disturbed, flashes of light are a common experience.

Hearing 'sounds' when none is actually present can trigger quite severe additional symptoms because of the early warning effect continuing and the person remaining on alert (see box on page 89). Individuals can become on edge, bad tempered, irritable and unable to concentrate. If the onset of the tinnitus is associated with a bad event, such as an accident, an explosion, a whiplash injury, a family death, etc, this tends to accentuate its effect.

Other factors that raise the level of generalised brain-stem activity, such as anger, illness or tiredness when there is a need to remain alert, can all increase the awareness of the tinnitus and the distress that it is causing. Of course, thinking about the noises will tend to accentuate them.

This distress can start to affect individuals psychologically, depending on their characters and personality. Some people have ordered, structured lives over which they have perfect control and they get extremely angry when they simply cannot command their tinnitus to go away. The more they concentrate on making it disappear, the worse it can get, driving them to greater anger, especially at night time in the quiet. Many individuals get up, switch on the radio, television, washing machine or tumble drier to drown out the noise, or may even go out and pace the streets.

Others despair that their world will never be quiet again and fear that they will always have this 'noise' with them wherever they go, and they may fall into a deep depression. Yet more will have great difficulty sleeping, and this lack of sleep and the need to function the next day leave them exhausted, which often tends to enhance the perception of the tinnitus. Many individuals are scared that they may have a brain tumour or some other terminal disease that is showing itself first by this noise. Indeed, in centuries past, noises in the head were often thought to be work of the devil. All in all, individuals can be affected in many different adverse ways depending on the impact that the tinnitus has on them personally.

Not all tinnitus is enduring; most people who go to over-loud clubs or concerts develop tinnitus but soon the noises fade into the background and disappear. Some individuals have a relaxed, laid-back

The Medical Research Council's 1989 national survey of hearing found that 10 per cent of the population had tinnitus that lasted for more than five minutes.

About two per cent of the population had tinnitus that caused them moderate troubles.

As many as five per 1,000 – that is nearly one-third of a million people in the UK – had tinnitus that severely affected their quality of life.

personality and just accept the sounds as 'just another thing' or 'something to do with getting old', and quickly come to accept their noises.

TYPES AND CAUSES OF TINNITUS

The different types of tinnitus

The vast majority of people with tinnitus have noises that can be heard only by them (subjective tinnitus). There is, however, a small group who hear sounds that are also audible to others; they have what is called objective tinnitus. These sounds are frequently the result of blood flowing through rough and narrowed arteries and causing a whooshing sound as it tumbles through the stricture. Sometimes abnormalities of veins, either malformations or benign tumours growing in or close to the ear (glomus tumours), can cause a similar whooshing, pulsatile sound, which can often be heard with a stethoscope held over the carotid artery and/or jugular vein in the neck. A woman once came to my clinic because her dog kept lifting its ears and listening to her right ear. She had, it turned out, a carotid artery narrowing and the high-pitched sounds of the blood rushing through the narrowed artery could be heard by her dog!

Clicking noises can also arise from the ear and seem to come from irregular, tic-like contractions of the muscles of the palate (palatal myoclonus) or of the middle-ear muscles. This phenomenon is similar to a facial tic when some of the facial muscles twitch, but in this case the closeness of the affected muscles to the ear makes the twitching audible. Some surgeons have attempted to cure these clicks, which can be extremely irritating to the sufferer, by cutting the muscles in the middle ear themselves, but this is rarely successful.

People whose noises are not pulsatile and cannot be heard by others describe what they hear in a huge variety of ways, including buzzing, ringing, whining and probably every possible sound that has ever been described. These sounds can also be located just outside the ear, in one ear or the other or all over the head. This type of tinnitus is called subjective and is the most common form of the condition.

CAUSES OF SUBJECTIVE TINNITUS

The 'source' of most forms of subjective tinnitus is not understood. It is easy to blame the hair cells by saying that they are malfunctioning, and that instead of detecting sound they are mischievously generating electrical signals that are then perceived as sounds. Scientifically, it is difficult to show that this is actually the case and, although it may be true in some people, it cannot be used as a general explanation.

However, there are some specific causes of subjective tinnitus that need to be excluded. This applies especially to tinnitus localised to one ear when, among other causes, middle-ear and mastoid disease must be ruled out. Investigations include a physical

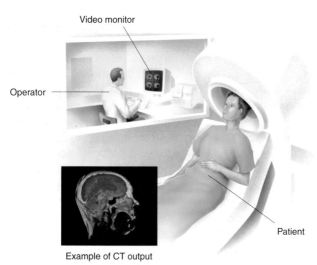

Video monitor

Operator

Patient

Example of CT output

Computed tomography (CT) fires X-rays through the brain at different angles. The X-rays are picked up by receivers and the information analysed by a computer to create a picture of the brain.

Example of MRI output

Magnetic resonance imaging (MRI) can detect many subtle and small abnormalities that are invisible to CT scanning.

examination, audiometry and appropriate imaging by computed tomography (CT) or magnetic resonance imaging (MRI).

Tinnitus in one ear associated with some distortion of hearing is occasionally caused by an acoustic neuroma (see page 68). This is more likely if there is a sensorineural hearing loss on the same side. The ideal way to find out whether a person has one of these benign but unpleasant tumours is to send him or her for MRI. This supplies sufficient detail to make certain that the person does not have any of the many other sorts of tumours and diseases in the head and, if this is the case, the tinnitus can be termed 'idiopathic' which, in effect, means without known cause – yet.

As technology improves and understanding of the mechanisms of tinnitus increases, the idiopathic group (without recognisable cause) – which is the majority at present – will probably get smaller as clear-cut causes will be found for many of those concerned. Once each clear-cut cause is defined, specific medical remedies should eventually become available.

However, at present for those people with idiopathic tinnitus without a hearing loss, all we can say is that somewhere along the line from cochlea to auditory cortex,

The body usually sets a hearing threshold that excludes internal 'body' noises. If this perceptual threshold drops, the 'body' noises can be heard, creating the effect of tinnitus.

No tinnitus

Sound must be greater than the perceptual threshold to be heard. Internal 'body' noise is less than the threshold and so is not heard

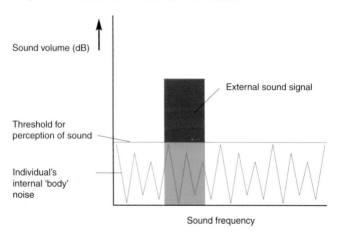

Tinnitus

Internal 'body' noise is now perceptible as a sound signal because the perceptual threshold signal has dropped

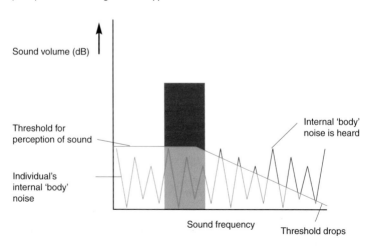

irregular electrical signals are being generated. For people with a hearing loss, alternative mechanisms to explain their tinnitus have been proposed and this is how the argument goes: from the hair cell in the cochlea inwards, the hearing system is an electrical network with relays, junctions, enhancing devices, filters, etc. Any electrical system has electrical 'noise' in it. It is easy to demonstrate this by having a hi-fi amplifier turned to full volume with no input such as a CD or tape playing and, even if the system is extremely expensive, there will still be some noise heard through the speakers.

There will always be background electrical noise in the auditory system; normally you don't hear this because your brain sets a threshold level that excludes it. For an incoming sound signal to be heard, it has to be greater than the background noise threshold. People have a wide range of hearing thresholds.

When a hearing loss occurs, whatever the cause, it may just be great enough to prevent normal external sounds reaching the brain. 'Silence' over the range of pitches represented by the deafness is therefore registered by the brain. The world is not a silent place – it may be quiet but silence is extremely difficult to achieve – and the absence of sound means that our early warning system cannot register change. The brain therefore reacts by dropping the threshold to 'hear' more, and by doing so strays into the internal noise levels so that the individual is hearing the workings of his or her own ear.

If placed in a totally silent space (an anechoic chamber) for experimental purposes, most people with normal hearing develop tinnitus, which slowly goes away when they return to a normal, noisy environment. This effect will recur each time the experiment is repeated, but most people do not like the sensation of total silence because it gives them an uneasy, frightened feeling. This is presumably because they no longer have 'hearing' as their early warning system and they feel vulnerable at a primitive animal brain-stem level.

HOW THE BRAIN DEALS WITH CONTINUING EXTERNAL NOISES

Most of us have had the experience of sitting in a room, concentrating on something such as reading or writing, and then hearing the clock stop when we hadn't previously noticed it ticking. Now, as the clock has stopped, there is actually nothing to hear but, previously, the brain stem filtered out the harmless repetitive noise of its ticking so that the sound did not reach the level of perception. This is more difficult to do with an irregular dripping tap, which can be a source of continued annoyance, partly because we tend to anticipate the arrival of the next drip and experience further brain-stem consternation when the sound does not occur.

Depending on the personality of the individual, he or she either learns to tolerate the irregularity or eventually gets furious and does something about it. The same thing occurs when you buy a new refrigerator. Initially the noise of it switching on and off in an irregular fashion and of the motor running can be irritating. Eventually, however, almost everyone gets used to it and it stops being a problem.

The brain stem has awesome powers of processing incoming auditory signals. It can filter out those that it recognises as harmless in the light of experience. The early warning effect and all the additional emotional factors associated with unexplained and unexpected sounds do not arise, and the signal may eventually not even reach consciousness.

Humans have loaded on top of this complex survival computer an additional 'higher level' computer bank, which gives us sensations, feelings, thoughts and emotions that can, in turn, interact and influence the lower centres. The stage is thus set, in susceptible individuals, for an internal conflict with slightly unusual electrical activity in the auditory system awakening fear and anxiety in the 'higher-level' computer bank; this feeds back to promote general arousal of the brain stem and consequent distress. It is irrelevant whether the sounds are external or internal – the process remains the same.

DISRUPTION OF CONCENTRATION

Language is a very high-level skill and we use considerable brain power to understand speech. You can concentrate on only one conversation at a time and, although you may hear other voices going on around you, they are only sounds – you cannot understand the full sense. Almost everyone is familiar with the scene at a party when you are in deep conversation with some friends and there is a general babble around you. Someone behind your back mentions your name, which you hear, and immediately you shift the focus of your attention to this new and interesting sound. In doing so, you completely lose track of the first conversation.

Tinnitus is an attention thief. The unexplained sound tries to grab your attention. It is saying 'Listen to me – I may be important' and keeps distracting your brain from whatever it is doing at the time. People with tinnitus often have major difficulties in coping with complex mental tasks because of this unwelcome and persistent attention-grabber.

HELPING PEOPLE WITH TINNITUS

People who develop tinnitus can suffer serious distress and even psychiatric problems, including depression, anxiety and sometimes suicidal thoughts. Fortunately most people are not so severely affected and are referred by their GP to the ENT department of their local hospital.

At such a clinic, the ENT consultant will ask you questions to determine the nature of your problem and any associated symptoms. If your symptoms suggest that you may have problems arising from local disease in your ear, nose and throat, your central nervous system or the major blood vessels of your neck, you will have a very thorough examination.

A pure-tone audiogram will probably be performed and, depending on the results and your symptoms, further investigations may be undertaken. In this way, the rare specific causes of tinnitus can be diagnosed and referred for appropriate treatment. For the vast majority of people, however, the tests will show that there is nothing life threatening or otherwise seriously wrong, and your doctor can be quite confident of this, whatever you may have feared. Such reassurance about the nature of the problem helps to allay inner fears, which are a potent source of the anxiety that keeps the tinnitus active. The next step is to find ways of managing the problem.

The aim of tinnitus management is to relieve the brain-stem 'distress' that comes with the sounds. The brain stem can be helped to 'learn' that the sounds are not a threat and that they can eventually be disregarded (acclimatisation), so that they no longer reach consciousness or activate the early warning effect. In many people, a careful examination, appropriate investigations and a clearly reasoned explanation are enough to set the process of acclimatisation in progress. However, the interaction between the higher centres of the brain and the brain stem are complex and poorly understood. Other people may need more help, depending on the severity and intrusiveness of their sounds and on their personality.

People with significant hearing loss

Restoration of hearing, usually with a hearing aid, often overcomes tinnitus by allowing the brain's hearing threshold to be reset, so that the tinnitus is no longer heard. This is the best result. Sometimes, restoring hearing is not immediately effective, but the level of the tinnitus drops significantly so that the internal sounds become less important in relation to newly heard external sounds.

Most forms of acoustic management of tinnitus now work in this way. Sounds are introduced to reduce the importance of the internal sounds, so that the brain stem 'learns' to push the tinnitus into the background and then into insignificance. Using loud sounds to drown out the tinnitus completely is known as full masking, but this is not now thought to be the best form of management; when the masking is removed, the tinnitus may still be present at the same level.

'Masking' techniques: sound generators

Hearing aids can be modified to incorporate a sound generator that produces an appropriate suppressing sound, perhaps wide-band white noise (a 'shushing' sound) at half the full-masking level. This combination is very effective in people with tinnitus and hearing loss if pure amplification is not enough to reduce the tinnitus level. Once the tinnitus levels have diminished, the degree of distress associated with them also lessens and the brain stem learns to filter out the intrusive sounds.

Pure masking devices set at half-masking levels are frequently helpful for those with normal hearing. The introduction of a not-unpleasant background sound provides a distraction, so that the primary 'warning' effects of the tinnitus start to diminish, and eventually the tinnitus stops being an irritation and is no longer heard.

Environmental aids

Many people find that getting to sleep in a quiet environment is a real problem. For these people, quiet environmental sounds, such as having a radio playing or a cassette with their favourite music or even something like an audio-book, are sometimes a great help. Some people find the low drone of speech quite soporific, whereas others listen to the sense and so cannot get to sleep. Everyone has his or her own special way of dealing with the problem, and some experimentation may be needed. Partners may get irritated by the chosen noise (in much the same way that tinnitus irritates the sufferer), but you can get pillow loudspeakers that can be heard only when your head is on your pillow and not by anyone else. Many high street electrical shops sell these relatively cheaply but in case of difficulty the RNID has a list of suppliers (see Useful addresses).

Quiet environmental sounds can also be used to relax you during the daytime. Many people who would normally work, read or do other things, such as knitting, in the quiet find that, once they have tinnitus, they need to have music playing in the background. There are now several useful tapes that provide soothing sounds, such as the waves of the sea, to help. The RNID can advise on where to buy these if your local audiology clinic or hearing aid centre cannot help.

PSYCHOLOGICAL HELP AND COGNITIVE THERAPY

Although the techniques described above help most people to manage their tinnitus, there is a minority whose personality makes it difficult for them to tolerate this imperfection, or who cannot accept that there is something in their lives that they are unable to control. These people need additional help, because they tend to concentrate on the tinnitus in an attempt to make it disappear. This is like trying to make yourself go to sleep – you cannot succeed in this, you simply fall asleep despite your efforts. In trying to make 'nothing' happen it becomes 'something' and this philosophy applies to tinnitus exactly.

Distraction is needed, and various relaxation techniques are useful in deflecting concentration away from the tinnitus. These techniques usually need to be taught by hearing therapists or people who are trained in the techniques. Most NHS audiology departments or hearing aid centres have hearing therapists trained in these techniques. There are many relaxation tapes and yoga-type exercises that help people who are already using sound substitution devices such as maskers, hearing aids, pillow speakers, etc. Indeed, effective relaxation therapy alone may be enough to overcome the tinnitus-related distress.

There are also some simple techniques or tricks to help at night if tinnitus either stops you falling asleep or prevents you from dropping off again when you wake during the night. First, do not look at the clock. Next, do not get up and make a cup of tea or coffee. These actions bring awareness and the stimulants in tea or coffee prolong this. Find a simple word – I like rich-sounding words such as 'implosion' or 'cartridge' – and gently repeat them again and again with different emphasis.

People become deeply entwined with their tinnitus so that it becomes a focus of their lives, taking over most minutes of every day. They find that they cannot let go of the symptom, which comes to dominate them. Cognitive therapy is a technique directed at altering the way in which people think about their symptoms.

Imagine standing in a stuffy, noisy, crowded underground train. You are packed shoulder to shoulder, you cannot move and you cannot turn your head it is so crowded. Then you start to feel someone behind you poking you in the ribs with what must be a sharpish object as it is very painful. This is an irregular but recurring event. What do you feel? Pain, of course, but also anger, resentment, and fear perhaps, but why? People give many different reasons. They may feel out of control, threatened, invaded, that the other individual is so selfish and so on – you may have other thoughts.

Eventually the train reaches the station and enough people get off to allow you to turn around and speak your mind. As you turn you see that the person behind is a blind man and that it is his white stick that has been prodding you. Now what do you feel? I am sure it is not the same as before.

The essence of the plot is that symptoms (tinnitus/pain/dizziness, etc.) engender feelings (anger/frustration/fear) because of the way we think about them. Cognitive therapy aims to alter that link between symptoms and feelings so that the symptoms become 'acceptable'. Once they do the symptoms tend to evaporate. Cognitive therapy for tinnitus is a specialist skill that is available within the NHS, although the provision of services is very patchy. I refer you to some excellent short books by my colleagues, which are in the reading list on page 105.

SURGERY FOR TINNITUS

Avoid surgery for tinnitus like the plague. Tinnitus is a symptom and surgery is performed for conditions that give rise to symptoms. Since virtually all forms of tinnitus are without a truly known cause, surgical procedures claiming to be curative are not logical. The emotional effect of a major operation may displace the symptoms of tinnitus. The pain of surgery may act as a 'masker' much as acupuncture helps relieve tinnitus while it is in use. However, performing operations to 'cut the cochlear nerve to prevent the hair cells from sending tinnitus signals to the brain' simply does not work and may even make individuals worse, because a dead ear cannot be helped by hearing aids, sound generators or environmental aids.

Some conditions have tinnitus as part of their presentation. Examples are otosclerosis and acoustic neuromas. Indeed the tinnitus may well improve after successful surgery to restore the hearing in otosclerosis and may become much less marked after acoustic neuroma surgery with hearing preservation. However, it is an unwise surgeon who promises that the tinnitus will get better in these specific conditions; if it does then that is an unexpected bonus.

KEY POINTS

✓ Tinnitus is hearing a sound when none is present in the environment

✓ Tinnitus can be subjective or, rarely, objective when another person can hear the sounds in the individual's ear

✓ Tinnitus can evoke many unpleasant sensations but it is only rarely caused by serious underlying disease

✓ Most tinnitus fades into insignificance and becomes unobtrusive with time

✓ Tinnitus in one ear, especially if it is associated with a hearing loss, needs investigation

✓ Management of tinnitus involves exclusion of underlying disease, treatment of any hearing loss, explanation, counselling, and sometimes a masker and/or hearing aid

✓ Overall, and for most people, natural compensation occurs but this can be helped with good and kindly advice

Useful addresses

Benefits Enquiry Line
Tel: 0800 882200
Minicom: 0800 243355
Website: www.dwp.gov.uk
N. Ireland: 0800 220674

Government agency giving information and advice on sickness and disability benefits for people with disabilities and their carers.

British Acoustic Neuroma Association
Oak House
Ransom Wood Business Park
Southwell Road West
Mansfield
Nottinghamshire NG21 0HJ
Tel: 01623 632143
Fax: 01623 635313
Helpline: 0800 652 3143
Email: bana@ukan.freeserve.co.uk
Website: www.ukan.co.uk/bana

Offers information sheets, audio tapes and videos about acoustic neuroma. Has local branches and can put people in touch with each other for mutual support in coping with this disorder.

British Academy of Audiology
(Merging of British Association of Audiological Society, British Association of Audiologists and British Society of Hearing Therapists)
PO Box 346
Peterborough PE6 7EG
Tel: 01733 253976
Email: admin@baaudiology.org
Website: www.baaudiology.org

Professional body representing and advising health professionals working in the field of audiology.

British Tinnitus Association (BTA)
Unit 5, Ground Floor
Acorn Business Park
Woodseats Close
Sheffield S8 0TB
Tel: 0114 250 9922
Fax: 0114 258 2279
Helpline: 0800 018 0527
Minicom: 0114 250 9922
Email: info@tinnitus.org.uk
Website: www.tinnitus.org.uk

Acts as umbrella for nation-wide support groups and has information about tinnitus. Offers training to health professionals.

Council for Advancement of Communication with Deaf People (CACDP)
Durham University Science Park

Block 4
Stockton Road
Durham DH1 3UZ
Tel: 0191 383 1155
Fax: 0191 383 7914
Text: 0191 383 7915
Email: durham@cacdp.org.uk
Website: www.cacdp.org.uk

Examination Board for British sign language and other deaf studies qualifications. Holds register of interpreters.

Cued Speech Association UK
9 Duke Street
Dartmouth
Devon TQ6 9PY
Tel: 01803 832784
Fax: 01803 835311
Text: 01803 832784
Email: info@cuedspeech.co.uk
Website: www.cuedspeech.co.uk

Offers information, support and training for parents and professionals about cued speech. This lip-reading supplement can provide complete spoken language through vision for deaf people. Publications and videos available.

Deaf Education through Listening and Talking (DELTA)
PO Box 20
Haverhill
Suffolk CB9 7BD
Tel: 01440 783689
Fax: 01440 783689
Email: enquiries@deafeducation.org.uk
Website: www.deafeducation.org.uk

National group of teachers and parents of deaf children offering information and guidance to help children develop normal speech and live independently. Runs conferences for professionals and summer schools for families.

Defeating Deafness (The Hearing Research Trust)
330–332 Gray's Inn Road
London WC1X 8EE
Tel: 020 7833 1733
Fax: 020 7278 0404
Helpline: 0808 808 2222
Textphone: 020 7915 1412
Email: contact@defeatingdeafness.org
Website: www.defeatingdeafness.org

The only UK charity dedicated to funding medical research into hearing impairment. Offers information service on hearing-related illnesses.

Disability Rights Commission
FREEPOST
MID 02164
Stratford upon Avon CV37 9BR
Tel: 0845 762 2633
Fax: 0845 777 8878
Textphone: 0845 762 2644
Email: enquiries@drc-gb.org
Website: www.drc-gb.org

Government sponsored centre offering publications and up-to-date information on the Disability Discrimination Act. Special team of advisers can help with problems of discrimination at work.

Hearing Aid Council
Witan Court
305 Upper Fourth Street
Central Milton Keynes
Bucks MK9 1EH
Tel: 01908 235700
Fax: 01908 233770
Email: hac@thehearingaidcouncil.org.uk
Website:
www.thehearingaidcouncil.org.uk

Regulatory body reporting to the Department of Trade and Industry. Provides rules on code of practice to dispensers and their employees of non-NHS, privately available hearing aids.

Hearing Concern

4th Floor
275–281 King Street
London W6 9LZ
Tel: 020 8233 2929
Fax/Text: 020 8233 2934
Helpline: 0845 074 4600
Email: info@hearingconcern.org.uk
Website: www.hearingconcern.org.uk

Offers advice and support to hard-of-hearing and deaf adults and professionals. Trained volunteers around the UK are available to visit people's homes to give advice. Arranges holidays designed for people with hearing loss and their relatives and friends.

Hearing Dogs for Deaf People

The Grange
Wycombe Road
Saunderton, Princes Risborough
Bucks HP27 9NS
Tel: 01844 348100 (voice and minicom)
Fax: 01844 348101
Email: info@hearing-dogs.co.uk
Website: www.hearing-dogs.co.uk

Selects and trains rescue dogs. Voluntary branches across the UK.

LINK Centre for Deafened People

19 Hartfield Road
Eastbourne
East Sussex BN21 2AR
Tel: 01323 638230
Fax: 01323 642968
Text: 01323 739998
Email: info@linkdp.org
Website: www.linkcentre.org

Provides a comprehensive rehabilitation service for deafened adults and their families. Offers training to health professionals and deafened people working together. Referrals by health professionals necessary.

Menière's Society

The Rookery
Surrey Hills Business Park
Wotton
Dorking RH5 6QT
Tel/Text: 01306 876883
Fax: 01306 876057
Helpline: 0845 120 2975
Email: info@menieres.org.uk
Website: www.menieres.org.uk

Offers general information about Menièère's disease and how to manage it. Members can be put in touch with others in order to share coping strategies.

National Centre for Deaf Blindness

John and Lucille Van Geest Place
8 Cygnet Road
Hampton
Peterborough PE7 8FD
Tel: 01733 358100
Fax: 01733 358356
Text: 01733 358858
Helpline: 0800 132320
Email: info@deafblind.org.uk
Website: www.deafblind.org.uk

Membership organisation that offers information and training to staff, sufferers and their families as well as support. Training available to other organisations. Transcribing services also provided.

National Deaf Children's Society (NDCS)

15 Dufferin Street
London EC1Y 8UR
Tel: 020 7490 8656
Fax: 020 7251 5020
Helpline and minicom: 0808 800 8880
Text: 020 7490 8656
Email: ndcs@ndcs.org.uk
Website: www.ndcs.org.uk

National organisation providing support in the home with advice on education, aids, etc. Runs workshops, holds exhibitions and provides training for professionals.

National Institute for Health and Clinical Excellence (NICE)
MidCity Place
71 High Holborn
London WC1V 6NA
Tel: 020 7067 5800
Fax: 020 7067 5801
Email: nice@nice.nhs.uk
Website: www.nice.org.uk

Provides national guidance on the promotion of good health and the prevention and treatment of ill-health. Patient information leaflets are available for each piece of guidance issued.

Royal National Institute for Deaf People (RNID)
19–23 Featherstone Street
London EC1Y 8SL
Tel: 020 7296 8000
Fax: 020 7296 8199
Helpline: 0808 808 0123
Text: 0808 808 9000
Email: informationline@rnid.org.uk
Website: www.rnid.org.uk

A key player in providing a variety of information for the deaf and hard of hearing, in establishing new services, campaigning for equality at all levels and developing awareness of the issues at the highest level.

Sense, The National Deafblind and Rubella Association
11–13 Clifton Terrace
Finsbury Park
London N4 3SR
Tel: 020 7272 7774
Fax: 020 7272 6012

Text: 020 7272 9648
Email: info@sense.org.uk
Website: www.sense.org.uk

Offer general information, support and training for families of deaf–blind people and care workers. Has local support groups.

Sign Community (British Deaf Association, BDA)
1–3 Worship Street
London EC2A 2AB
Tel: 020 7588 3520
Fax: 020 7588 3527
Helpline voice phone: 0870 770 3300
Helpline minicom: 0800 652 2965
Videophone: 020 7496 9539
Email: helpline@signcommunity.org.uk
Website: www.signcommunity.org.uk

Offers information, counselling services and promotes the use of sign language run by deaf people for deaf people.

FURTHER READING

Deafness, 6th edn. Edited by J. Graham and M.C. Martin, 2001. London: Whurr Publications. ISBN 1-870332-23-7

A good book dealing in greater depth, written for all those groups dealing with people with deafness.

Diseases of the Ear, 6th edn. Edited by H. Ludman and T. Wright, 1998, London: Arnold. ISBN 0-340-56441-7

A book written for ENT surgeons in training, which goes into most aspects of the causes and management of deafness and tinnitus in great depth.

Living with Tinnitus. R. Hallam, Wellingborough: Thorsons Publishers. ISBN 0-7225-1801-3

A really very useful book from a recognised authority with lots of useful tips. Out of print but most libraries have or can get copies.

Tinnitus: when silence is a stranger. L. Sheppard, 1993. Wingfield, Norfolk: The Norfolk Tinnitus Society. ISBN 0-9520642-1-9

Another very helpful book with lots of useful information.

The Forest Bookshop specialises in deafness and deaf issues and publishes an extensive mail order catalogue. The address is:
8 St John Street
Coleford
Glos GL16 8AR
Tel: 01594 833858
Email: deafbooks@forestbook.com
Website: www.ForestBooks.com

THE INTERNET AS A SOURCE OF FURTHER INFORMATION

After reading this book, you may feel that you would like further information on the subject. One source is the internet and there are a great many websites with useful information about medical disorders, related charities and support groups. Some websites, however, have unhelpful and inaccurate information. Many are sponsored by commercial organisations or raise revenue by advertising, but nevertheless aim to provide impartial and trustworthy health information. Others may be reputable but you should be aware that they may be biased in their recommendations. Remember that treatment advertised on international websites may not be available in the UK.

Unless you know the address of the specific website that you want to visit (for example, familydoctor.co.uk), you may find the following guidelines helpful when searching the internet.

There are several different sorts of websites that you can use to look for information, the main ones being search engines, directories and portals.

Search engines and directories

There are many search engines and directories that all use different algorithms (procedures for computation) to return different results when you do a search. Search engines use computer programs called spiders, which crawl the web on a daily basis to search individual pages within a site and then queue them ready for listing in their database.

Directories, however, consider a site as a whole and use the description and information that was provided with the site when it was submitted to the directory to decide whether a site matches the searcher's needs. For both there is little or no selection in terms of quality of information, although engines and directories do try to impose rules about decency and content. Popular search engines in the UK include:

> google.co.uk
> aol.co.uk
> msn.co.uk
> lycos.co.uk
> hotbot.co.uk
> overture.com
> ask.co.uk
> espotting.com
> looksmart.co.uk
> alltheweb.com
> uk.altavista.com

The two biggest directories are:

> yahoo.com
> dmoz.org

Portals

Portals are doorways to the internet that provide links to useful sites, news and other services, and may also provide search engine services (such as msn.co.uk). Many portals charge for putting their clients' sites high up in your list of search results. The quality of the websites listed depends on the selection criteria used in compiling the portal, although portals focused on a specific group, such as medical

information portals, may have more rigorous inclusion criteria than other searchable websites. Examples of medical portals can be found at:

> nhsdirect.nhs.uk
> patient.co.uk

Links to many British medical charities will be found at the Association of Medical Research Charities (www.amrc.org.uk) and Charity Choice (www.charitychoice. co.uk).

Search phrases

Be specific when entering a search phrase. Searching for information on 'cancer' could give astrological information as well as medical: 'lung cancer' would be a better choice. Either use the engine's advanced search feature and ask for the exact phrase, or put the phrase in quotes – 'lung cancer' – as this will link the words. Adding 'uk' to your search phrase will bring up mainly British websites, so a good search would be 'lung cancer' uk (don't include uk within the quotes).

Always remember that the internet is international and unregulated. Although it holds a wealth of invaluable information, individual websites may be biased, out of date or just plain wrong. Family Doctor Publications accepts no responsibility for the content of links published in their series.

Index